A NEW LOOK AT AN OLD EARTH

DON STONER

HARVEST HOUSE PUBLISHERS
Eugene, Oregon 97402

Cover by Garborg Design Works, Minneapolis, Minnesota

A NEW LOOK AT AN OLD EARTH

Copyright ©1985, 1986, 1987, 1988, 1991, 1992, 1996, 1997 by Donald Wayne Stoner
Published by Harvest House Publishers
Eugene, Oregon 97402

Library of Congress Cataloging-in-Publication Data

Stoner, Donald Wayne
    A new look at an old earth / Don Stoner.
        p.   cm.
    Includes bibliographical references and indexes.
    ISBN 1-56507-595-1
    1. Bible and science.   2. Earth—Age.   3. Hermeneutics.
    4. Science—Philosophy.   5. Bible. O.T. Genesis I—Criticism.
    Interpretation, etc. 6. Creationism.   I. Title.
    BS650.S735 1997   231.7'.652—dc21   96-45433
                                                                CIP

97 98 99 00 01 02 03 / BP / 10 9 8 7 6 5 4 3 2 1

Acknowledgments

There are too many people—scientists and theologians, old earthers and young earthers—who have helped with this project to list them all here, and I fear I may forget someone if I try. Still, I would like to make one mention: It is the intent that this book be comprehensible to a tired mother of five at 11 p.m. at the end of a hard day. I would like to thank my wife, Debbie, for providing the feedback to make this goal possible.

About the Author

Don Stoner was introduced to the controversy surrounding Genesis in the second grade when he came home from school and asked his father why he was taught in Sunday school that the earth was created in six days and in elementary school that it was created over a much greater period of time. Fortunately, answers were available; his grandfather, Peter W. Stoner, was the author of *Science Speaks,* a bestseller on the subject of scientific proof of the inerrancy of prophecy and the Bible. The subject has fascinated Don since, and over the years he has become an authority on the subject of creation.

Don went on to receive his B.S. in physics and has been awarded two U.S. patents. Two of the more notable projects he has been involved with professionally include the development of the optical disc and the Precision Motion Chiptester. Don and his wife, Debbie, have four daughters and one son.

Contents

FOREWORD
by Dr. Hugh Ross

James, the brother of Jesus, in addressing the council at Jerusalem declared, "It is my judgment, therefore, that we should not make it difficult for the Gentiles who are turning to God" (Acts 15:19). The apostle Paul in his letter to the Romans said, "Make up your mind not to put any stumbling block or obstacle in your brother's way" (Romans 14:13). Don Stoner challenges us in the following pages to remove a great impediment to the furtherance of the gospel of Jesus Christ.

Instead of focusing on the now overwhelming evidence for the God of the Bible and on the complete accuracy of His Word, many within Christendom would have us discount this potent new evidence, all for the sake of clinging to the rather peripheral (to the gospel) dogma of a recently created universe.

This digression has effectively inoculated a large segment of secular society against taking seriously the call to faith in Christ. It also has divided the Christian community into hostile camps that focus more energy on attacking each other than on reaching nonbelievers. Worse yet, the nation's courts have come to perceive age as the central issue for the creation/evolution debate. Thus, a pretext has been provided— the lack of credibility for a thousands-of-years-old universe— for removing the Bible and the concept of creation from public education.

As Mr. Stoner emphasizes, science is man's attempt to interpret the facts of nature, while theology is man's attempt to interpret the words of the Bible. God created the universe and also is responsible for the words of the Bible. Since He is incapable of lying or deceit, there can be no contradiction between the words of the Bible and the facts of nature. Any conflict between science and theology must be attributable to human misinterpretation. Such conflicts should be welcomed, not feared or battled, for they point the way to further research and study that could resolve the apparent discrepancies.

Historically such resolutions have not only borne the fruit of bringing warring parties to peace and fellowship but also provided new tools for winning souls for Christ. It is in this spirit that this book is written, and it is in this spirit that I hope this book will be read.

PREFACE
by Chuck Smith Jr.
Senior Pastor, Capo Beach Calvary Chapel

As we grew up in Sunday school, our young minds were filled with wonderful stories about God and His work in the world. One of our lessons explained how Scripture clearly revealed that our entire universe was created in six days. I remember hearing about an usher (or a man named Ussher) who used biblical genealogies to calculate his way back to the first day of creation, which he determined must have occurred 6,000 years ago. Since all of his numbers added up mathematically, his dating had to be *scientifically* accurate.

At the same time, our minds were also filled with warnings about "scientists" whose chief aim was to discredit the Bible. Thus we were given the impression that a fundamental tension existed between science and Scripture. Like many other Christian youth, I thought I had to choose between science and God. The problem, as I came to conceive it, was that science strove to make sense of the universe, whereas the church demanded absolute faith in a *particular interpretation* of Scripture, regardless of scientific discoveries. If any discrepancy existed between science and our interpretation of the Bible, well, "Let God be true, and every man a liar" (Romans 3:4).

My reaction to evolution was probably normal, given my upbringing. There was simply no way life could emerge from inorganic materials apart from outside intervention, no matter how long the primordial soup was cooking on the cosmic stove. Even to this day I have not heard a compelling, scientific argument for biogenesis. On the other hand, the science teachers and professors we were supposed to watch out for were neither evil nor stupid. They did not persecute Christians or attack Scripture. But they did make a lot of sense. The universe they described was much older than the one we learned about in Sunday school, and the evidence they presented began to trouble me. Also troubling was the evidence of human cultures that existed more then 10,000 years ago. In high school I assumed orthodox Christianity demanded faith in a young universe, and the only reason scientists postulated that the universe had existed for billions of years was to accommodate evolutionary theories. Without scientific information to raise a real defense for a young earth, I retreated behind familiar Christian arguments and slogans. No believer had provided me with evidence for an alternative, such as, "God created the universe billions of years ago."

Sometimes the pressure of scientific discovery forces the church to reexamine its interpretation of Scripture and its assumptions about the universe. The sooner we realize we have come to a point of reevaluation, the sooner we can correct our thinking, ease the tension between faith and fact, and promote a stronger witness for God. The universe that exists is the universe God created. What does it tell us about itself and its Creator?

I am very grateful to Don Stoner for his sensitive treatment of this subject and his willingness to tackle such a controversial issue. His analysis and contribution to a biblical understanding of our universe will be a breath of fresh air to many Christians.

As Roman Catholic cardinals were afraid to look into Galileo's telescope for fear of what they might see, some closed-minded believers may choose not to take *A New Look At An Old Earth*. But those who do look are likely to learn some exciting truths about our God.

1

Judging
Ourselves First

Why do you look at the speck of sawdust in your
brother's eye and pay no attention to the plank in your
own eye? How can you say to your brother, "Let me take
the speck out of your eye," when all the time there is a
plank in your own eye? You hypocrite, first take the
plank out of your own eye, and then you will see clearly
to remove the speck from your brother's eye.

— MATTHEW 7:3-5

There is a passage of Scripture in Isaiah which describes a
beautiful condition of peace between all animals during the
millennium. This passage paints such a delightful mental
image that it is often the subject of pictures and statues. We
have all received greeting cards depicting this event with cute,
cuddly animals snuggled up next to each other in blissful dis-
regard for normal predator-prey relationships. We have all
heard preachers describe this scene to us. Hopefully, we have
even read this passage for ourselves, with our very own eyes
right out of our very own Bibles. Given this level of exposure,
we really ought to know what the Bible says about this familiar
scene. But do we? Let's test ourselves to find out: Does Isaiah
mention some predator which lies down with a lamb?

Which is more biblical? See Isaiah 11:6.

Most of us "remember" that the lion and lamb will lie down next to each other, but this is *not* what the Bible actually says! What Isaiah 11:6 says is:

> The *wolf* also shall dwell with the *lamb,* and the leopard shall *lie down* with the kid; and the calf and the young *lion* and the fatling together; and a little child shall lead them.
>
> —KJV, EMPHASIS ADDED; SEE ALSO ISAIAH 65:25

In fact, as a few minutes with a Bible and an exhaustive concordance will prove, the Bible *never* describes this scene exactly as most of us "remember" it. In our memories, where we thought we would find scriptural truth, we find instead a popular tradition—one which has gained entrance not by scriptural authority, but simply by persistent exposure to our senses.

There are many other traditional errors which gain unauthorized entry into our memories. For example, most of us "remember" that Jesus stumbled and fell while He was carrying His cross, but the Bible doesn't actually tell us this. We know that Jesus carried His own cross (John 19:17); we also know that Simon was forced to carry it (Matthew 27:32; Mark 15:21; Luke 23:26), but we can only speculate as to why Simon might have taken over. The Bible simply doesn't tell us this. For another example, although most of us "remember" that *Delilah* gave Samson his famous haircut, Scripture identifies the actual barber as "a man" in Judges 16:19.

It is easy to confuse what we have merely heard with what the Bible actually says; if we hear something often enough, we are even *likely* to become confused. We hear these things from people we trust and pass them on to others who trust us. We hardly ever stop to apply the scriptural admonition: "Test everything. Hold on to the good" (1 Thessalonians 5:21).

Still, this may not sound too important. It doesn't really matter whether or not Jesus actually stumbled while carrying His cross or how many types of animals will lie down in which combinations during the millennium. These questions are not really central to our faith, but are we any more careful when the questions *are* doctrinally significant?

Consider an example which relates to death as a consequence of sin. In the second chapter of Genesis, God gave one commandment which, in Adam's day, was all the biblical law that we find recorded:

> Of every tree of the garden thou mayest freely eat: But of the tree of the knowledge of good and evil, thou shalt not eat of it: for in the day that thou eatest thereof thou shalt surely die.
>
> —GENESIS 2:16,17 KJV

This single commandment was all Adam needed to understand and obey. Do we understand what this verse means? Did Adam really die in the day he sinned? The Bible tells us that he lived for many years after he ate the forbidden fruit (Genesis 5:3,4).

Most of us have heard from people we trust that Adam died *spiritually* rather than *physically* in the day he sinned, but how many of us have critically examined this interpretation to see if it is the truth? Because it is not a *literal* interpretation, we have good reason to be skeptical. To test this, the accepted method of comparing Scripture with Scripture must be applied.

There are several places in the Bible where death is referred to as a consequence of Adam's sin. For example, the Bible tells us Jesus had to die *physically* to atone for Adam's sin. As explained in the Gospels, there was no way the crucifixion could be avoided (see Matthew 26:39,42; Luke 24:20,26).

Romans 5:14 presents another place in Scripture where we can test the nature of Adam's curse:

> Nevertheless, death reigned from the time of Adam to the time of Moses, even over those who did not sin by breaking a command, as did Adam, . . .

Here Paul is using the obvious fact that all men between Adam and Moses died *physically* to prove his claim (in verse 12) that sin and human death entered through Adam. Notice that Paul considers these *physical* deaths to be such a clear effect of sin that their existence proves the presence of sin— even where no specific law has been broken. If this were not true, Paul's argument would be worthless; if Adam's sin brought only *spiritual* death, the *physical* deaths of all those men would prove nothing about sin's presence or absence.

God also confirmed that Adam's death would be physical when He pronounced the curse upon the ground after Adam's fall. As He explained to Adam in Genesis 3:19: " . . . for dust you are and to dust you will return."

Scripture teaches that Adam's sin brought *physical* death upon himself and upon all mankind and that Jesus had to die *physically* to atone for it. Whatever *spiritual* aspects might be involved, and regardless of their importance, related Scripture confirms the *physical* aspects. Where death is spoken of in Scripture as being the result of sin, the counsel of other Scripture teaches that *physical* death should be assumed irrespective of what decisions are made about *spiritual* death.[1]

The correct way to interpret Genesis 2:17 is that Adam was to die a literal, *physical* death in the day he ate the fruit. It is an accepted rule of interpretation that the *literal* meaning of a word in Scripture should be preferred over a *spiritual, figurative,* or *symbolic* one—especially when closely related passages confirm the *literal* meaning.

We still need to consider the problem that Adam did not die *physically* until long after he sinned. God's command places the execution of judgment within the same day as the act of disobedience. Might we be misunderstanding the word "day"?

The book of Genesis, like most of the Old Testament, was originally written in Hebrew. The word "day" was translated from the Hebrew word "yom." The *present-day* usage of our English word "day" is almost an exact equivalent of what "yom" meant back when Genesis was written.[2] It even carries the same alternate meanings. For example, both can mean: 24 hours; the 12 hours in which the sun is shining;* a moment of glory;** or a time period of indefinite length.*** When a person speaks of "the present day" (for example, in the third sentence of this paragraph) he is using the word "day" in the "indefinite period" sense. Notice that this usage is *literal,* not *figurative, symbolic,* or *spiritual.* The "present day" is not a poetic comparison to a 24-hour day; it is a *literal* time period of indefinite length. Likewise, the Bible sometimes uses the Hebrew "yom" in contexts referring to periods of greater length than 24 hours. For example, most of us believe that "the *day* of the Lord" (Isaiah 13:6,9) will last more than 24 hours.[3]

As we have seen, the related verses indicate that Adam died a *literal, physical* death in the "day" he sinned; it follows that the "day" in question must have been a time period of

---

* For example, "forty days and forty nights," Genesis 7:4.
** English example, "every dog has his day." Hebrew example, Hosea 7:5.
*** Genesis 2:4, for example, is normally assumed to refer to the whole creation period.

indefinite length. This very simple and quite *literal* understanding of the word "day" completely eliminates any problems.[4]

It is easy to be wrong, even about important verses, but at
least no real harm has been done here. Perhaps we were too
trusting when teachers we respect explained to us that Adam's
death was merely spiritual. Maybe those of us who have spread
this error should be more careful. Still, this error is not very
serious. Spreading it is not as harmful as spreading gossip—
where careless tales can cause real trouble.

This brings us to the reason for this book: Scientists who
are atheists are in error and need salvation as much as anyone
does. Showing Christians how to witness to them effectively is
one important goal of this book. Another goal is to show
Christians how to be more effective politically, so that they
might be able to correct some untrue "scientific" teachings
found in our public schools' curriculum. But before we correct others, we must apply Jesus' admonition in Matthew 7:3-5
(quoted at the beginning of this chapter) and remove the
errors from our own position.

Because our position is founded upon God's Word, the
Bible, we might assume we have made no errors. Unfortunately, as we have just seen, it is easier to make mistakes about
facts than we normally suppose—even about biblical facts. It
is all too easy to be wrong about what the Bible actually says.

It is routinely taught in evangelical Christian circles today
that the earth is very young—about 10,000 years old or even
younger. We hear this repeatedly from teachers we respect
and trust. We ourselves may have spread this teaching to those
who trust us. But is this teaching the biblical truth or is it an
error?

How old does the Bible say the earth is? The Genesis
account says it was created in six "days." But what does the
word "day" really mean? How long were the "days" of Genesis?
This is the same question we encountered regarding Adam's

fall in Genesis 2:17. Once again, a biblical "day" is not necessarily 24 hours long.

It is difficult to simply read the first chapter of Genesis and come away with any other meaning than six consecutive 24-hour days. But how much of this is because of the actual wording of Genesis and how much is because of what we have heard from others? Do the actual words of Genesis *really* make literal sense to us? "And there was evening, and there was morning—the first day" (Genesis 1:5). What could a literal "morning" possibly mean before the sun was made? (See Genesis 1:16.)

There is also the problem that the "plain English" which a modern reader encounters is not quite the same as the original Hebrew. Genesis might be harder to understand than we normally assume. The first chapter of Genesis is an ancient work; this can make it difficult to understand. Consider this verse from *The Faerie Queene*,[5] by Edmund Spenser, first published in A.D. 1590:

> A gentle Knight was pricking on the plaine, Ycladd in mightie armes and silver shielde, Wherein old dints of deepe woundes did remaine, The cruell markes of many' a bloody fielde; Yet armes till that time did he never wield. His angry steede did chide his foming bitt, As much disdayning *to the curbe to yield*: Full jolly knight he seemed, and faire did sitt, As one for knightly giusts and fierce encounters fitt.
>
> —BOOK 1, CANTO 1, VERSE 1, EMPHASIS ADDED

To a modern reader, the term "curbe" (curb in modern spelling) seems to mean something like a command to "halt." But this meaning makes the rest of that line confusing. The term actually refers to the horse's bit. In this example, the *correct* literal reading is not the plainest one! "Yielding to the curb" can even mean "being run off the road" in today's "plain English." This was written a mere 400 years ago and in an archaic form of *our own language,* yet it is still difficult to understand.

As we go back farther, our language gets even harder to understand. To the author of Beowulf, the first verse of Genesis looked something like this:[6]

On anginne gescēop God heofenan and eorðan.

This was written about 1,000 years ago in an archaic form of *our own language,* yet for most of us it is virtually impossible to read. However, Genesis was not written in English at all, but has been translated from Hebrew. The Hebrew language is very different from English. In Hebrew, Genesis 1:1 looks like this:[7]

בראשית ברא אלהים את השמים ואת הארץ׃

This text reads from right to left, has no vowels, and uses a very unfamiliar grammar which has no past, present, or future verb tense; it uses single-letter prefixes for the English words "in," "and," and "the," and also contains two short words which cannot be translated into English.[8] Does this look difficult? It gets worse—the Hebrew language has changed quite a bit over the last *several thousand years.* Here is the same verse as one authority believes it may have appeared in a very ancient form of Hebrew:[9]

𐤁𐤓𐤀𐤔𐤉𐤕 𐤁𐤓𐤀 𐤀𐤋𐤄𐤉𐤌 𐤀𐤕 𐤄𐤔𐤌𐤉𐤌 𐤅𐤀𐤕 𐤄𐤀𐤓𐤑

Furthermore, there is evidence that even this older form of Hebrew may have been a translation from a yet older account.[10] The real original was probably written even before the sun and moon were given proper names.[11] Notice that they are simply referred to as "great lights" in Genesis 1:16. It is difficult even to imagine an account of this antiquity.

Because we have difficulty understanding Edmund Spenser, who is relatively recent, we have no guarantee that a *plain reading* of Genesis 1 will give us an understanding which even remotely resembles the originally intended meaning. It is likely that we will have to be very careful if we hope to understand the creation account correctly.

Please notice that I am not saying that Scripture is *incomprehensible*, only that we must be careful if we are to understand it. The difficulties with ancient foreign languages are real and cannot be denied, but we must never use this as an excuse to abandon the authority of God's written Word in favor of our own opinions. If we can choose to deny the authority of even one word in the Bible, then *our choice* becomes the supreme authority rather than God's Word. This is obviously unacceptable.

As will be shown, there is an old-earth understanding of Genesis which is consistent with every detail in God's Word. We will have to keep our eyes open to see it, but it does not contradict Scripture. The young-earth point of view is *not* the only possible understanding of Genesis 1; in fact, as will also be shown, the young-earth position is incompatible with the scientific evidence which God's creation provides. I am not saying that God *couldn't* have created the world in six 24-hour periods; God is very powerful and can do just about anything. However, here we are *not* concerned with what God could have done, but with what He actually did.

Scientists can easily determine how old God's creation is. It speaks of its own age in many different ways. As will become obvious in following chapters, there is no escaping the antiquity of the earth. It is billions of years old. The scientific evidence is very clear. The Bible itself even seems to imply that a study of God's creation will reveal that the earth is *very* old:

> Since the creation of the world God's invisible qualities—his **eternal** power and divine nature—have been **clearly seen**, being understood from what has been made, so that men are without excuse.
>
> —ROMANS 1:20, EMPHASIS ADDED

God is *eternal* and powerful. His creation says so. Scientists have *clearly seen* the agelessness and power of God's creation from their own personal observations and measurements. They know who God must be.

What happens when we Christians tell scientists that the biblical text *cannot* be harmonized with an earth which is billions of years old? Scientists conclude that the God of the Bible is *not* the God of creation. This is because they have clearly seen God's creation and *we* have told them the biblical one is different! We have told them the Bible limits the age of the universe to about 10,000 years and they believe us—they *trust us* to understand the Bible and they take our word for what it says and means. Because they trust us, they will not bother to check the Scriptures for themselves. They simply conclude the biblical account is untrue.

Of course Romans 1:20 also says that scientists who do not recognize their Creator are "without excuse." Could it be that we are giving them one? If they trust us to give them an excuse to die in their sins, why won't they trust us for the whole truth? The problem is that we have failed to remove the "plank" from our own eye first. As Jesus told us in Matthew 7:3-5, we must fix our own eye before we can see clearly enough to fix our brother's eye. We must make sure we have the right understanding of what Genesis really means if we are to see clearly enough to correct the scientists. Any false assumptions we make will damage our attempts; if we are wrong, the scientists will know it and will not listen to us. As always, judgment should begin with the house of God (1 Peter 4:17).

Unfortunately, it is difficult for those who are not scientifically educated to tell the difference between scientific truth and error. An unsophisticated error will often be more alluring than the plain old truth. Because of this, we are unconsciously drawn to the wrong arguments. Juicy claims about how some Ph.D. has misread the facts are circulated from Christian to Christian just like gossip. We hear these stories from those we trust and pass them on to those who trust us. Unfortunately, we might never bother to find out if any of these stories are true.

As a result, we have been mocking educated men and, what is worse, we have done it from a position of ignorance. We have made fun of the fossil hunters, but how many of us have even held an authentic fossil in our own hands? We have called the men who dated those fossils fools, but how many of us would know how to date a fossil ourselves? Is knowledge about the stories we spread important or not? We must ask ourselves if *we* aren't really the fools. Does Solomon's description fit us?

> Wisdom calls aloud in the street, she raises her voice in the public squares; at the head of the noisy streets she cries out, in the gateways of the city she makes her speech: "How long will you simple ones love your simple ways? How long will mockers delight in mockery and fools hate knowledge? . . . "
>
> —PROVERBS 1:20-22

Even those of us who would never intentionally lie will thoughtlessly pass on almost anything we hear if it appears to glorify God. Sometimes we are much too gullible. We should always confirm information before we spread it to others. And how can we do this? Sorting truth from error requires careful testing. This cannot be accomplished by simply selecting those stories which please our ears. The truth is not always pleasant to hear!

Although it is necessary to expose the errors of the young-earth teaching, it can't be emphasized enough that the young-earth creationists and I are on the same side where it counts. As I will demonstrate, they are wrong about the age of the earth; however, we agree that God created everything and that knowing Him is the most important thing we can do. Perhaps the age of the earth should never have been made into an issue in the first place; unfortunately, it has been made into a serious one which must now be resolved. I apologize in advance for any hurt which I may inadvertently cause; it is my hope to restore unity among Christians, not to fuel division.

2

Science, Theology, and Truth

Test everything. Hold on to the good.

—1 Thessalonians 5:21

One goal of this book is to prepare Christians to lead scientists to Christ. In order to accomplish this, we must first remove the "plank" from our own eye. This means the young-earth position must be refuted (see chapters 3, 4, and 5). Another goal is to present biblical creationism in the context of an old universe (chapter 7). A third goal is to better acquaint Christians with their Creator by bringing them to a better understanding of His creation. These are ambitious undertakings to say the least.

Because readers are not expected to be scientifically educated, scientific information will be presented and explained as it becomes necessary for understanding. This book will gradually become more technical as it proceeds; by the end of this book, you should be properly prepared to present your faith to non-Christian scientists.

Let's start by reviewing the meanings of a few basic terms. Even with so modest a first step, you are likely to be in for a surprise or two. Consider the two terms "scientist" and "Christian." These are sometimes thought of as opposites—which they most certainly are *not*. A person who is a scientist is not necessarily a non-Christian and vice versa. The world is comprised of: Christians who are also scientists, Christians who are not scientists, scientists who are not Christians, and amazingly, people who are neither scientists nor Christians.

This carries an important consequence: Just because a teaching is scientific does not make it non-Christian! Scientists are *not always wrong*. Just because a scientist (even one who happens to be an atheist) believes that water freezes at 32 degrees Fahrenheit does not mean that Christians must believe otherwise. Likewise, just because a scientist (even one who happens to be an atheist) believes the earth is old does *not* mean that Christians must believe it is young. It is not necessary to disagree about everything.

Next, consider four more basic terms: 1) theology, 2) science, 3) the Bible, and 4) the universe. These terms relate as follows:

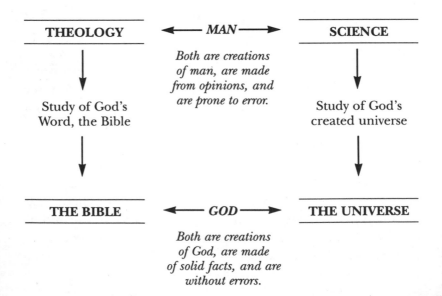

THEOLOGY	← *MAN* →	**SCIENCE**
↓	*Both are creations of man, are made from opinions, and are prone to error.*	↓
Study of God's Word, the Bible		Study of God's created universe
↓		↓
THE BIBLE	← *GOD* →	**THE UNIVERSE**
	Both are creations of God, are made of solid facts, and are without errors.	

Of course this diagram is not entirely complete—among other things, it ignores the spiritual realm and the fact that the Bible itself makes statements about the physical universe—but it will serve to demonstrate a few things.

For example, a scientist must have faith in the facts concerning the universe in exactly the same sense that a theologian is expected to have faith in God's Word, the Bible. The universe supplies evidence to support scientific theories, but what assurance does a scientist have that this evidence is valid—or that the universe will tell him the same story tomorrow? It is not difficult to imagine a universe with *invalid* evidence; most of us dream in one every night. A scientist's belief that the universe will tell him the truth must, in the final analysis, be taken on faith.

Likewise, a theologian should always regard his biblical theories with the same sense of skepticism with which a scientist is expected to regard scientific theories; he can be wrong about the Bible just like a scientist can be wrong about the universe. Even his cherished rules of biblical interpretation are fallible creations of men; they must *never* be confused with God's Word itself. If it were impossible to interpret Scripture incorrectly, there would be no false doctrines among us; there would not even be different denominations!

When a theologian tries to compare the Bible with science, what is he really doing? The two terms which he selects, "science" and "the Bible," provide a clue; the comparison is not a symmetrical one (the subtitle of this book provides an example of this). The theologian studies the Bible directly but he views the universe indirectly through science. He correctly regards the Bible as being inerrant and science as comprising opinions; at any point of conflict, he will side with the Bible. A theologian who is not scientifically educated may even favor his fallible rules of interpretation over the universe's solid physical evidence.

Now when a scientist makes a similar comparison, he does so from a different vantage point. He studies the universe directly but tends to get his information about the Bible indirectly through theology. He correctly regards the universe as being inerrant (meaning it is *real* and it transcends human opinions about it) and theology as comprising opinions. Naturally he will resolve all conflicts in favor of the universe. Adding further complication to this picture, a "pure" scientist should not begin with any presuppositions as to whether or not the Bible contains valid data; of course scientists who are either Christian or atheistic will unavoidably have such presuppositions. A scientist who is an atheist will naturally place his fallible theories above the Bible's inerrant text.

Considering this difference in approach, it is not too surprising that both theologians and scientists sometimes consider each other to be a little foolish; they both think their own position is founded upon solid evidence while the other's is based upon mere human opinions. Problems even arise between those scientists who acknowledge that the Bible is God's Word and those theologians who believe that God's universe speaks the truth.

What both the theologian and the scientist often fail to realize is that they are usually comparing theological theories about the Bible with scientific theories about the universe. When it comes to our general understanding of things, facts simply do not speak for themselves; they must be interpreted in the light of theory. The resulting disagreements are not too surprising, as both sides will often make errors.

If the Bible could be compared directly with the physical universe (the bare scientific facts), there should never be any disagreements. Unfortunately, this is difficult to do. In order to have a useful understanding of either the Bible or the universe, theories must be formed by which the various facts are understood and interpreted—for example: the doctrine of the Trinity (to explain apparent contradictions in the nature of God) or the theory of relativity (to explain apparent contradictions in the nature of time and space). Whenever theories are devised, mistakes are possible.

Theories, Facts, and Errors

There are no scientific "scriptures" (other than the universe itself) to guide scientists, so they have worked out their own system, which they call the scientific method. It is similar to the methods of interpretation that theologians have worked out to help them understand the Holy Scriptures. There is nothing sacred about the scientific method or about the methods theologians use. Both are fallible creations of men. Neither is recorded in God's Bible nor in His physical universe. They are merely well-thought-out tools which are useful in seeking after truth.

In principle, the task of a scientist is to study the world around him in order to figure out the rules which govern its events. There is an old joke about a scientist who is studying a frog. He has trained this frog to jump on command. When he says, "Frog jump!" the frog jumps. He then cuts off the frog's legs and repeats the command. The frog does not jump. The scientist concludes that the legless frog did not hear the command—that it must, therefore, hear with its legs.

This joke illustrates a difficulty with scientific inquiry. There is usually more than one possible explanation for the same observable facts. Sorting the right explanation from the wrong ones can require many well-designed experiments. Typically, the scientific method involves many cycles of looking at the evidence, formulating rules to describe the evidence, making predictions based on those rules, and then looking at the evidence again to see if the predictions were correct.[1] The more often this cycle is repeated, the more confident a scientist can be that he understands what he is studying.

No matter how many experiments are performed, scientists can never be absolutely sure about any of their conclusions. In fact, our scientist might remove the legs from a dozen frogs and still not know the truth. Even if he had been removing ears instead of legs, he could not be certain that he was not disabling the frog's ability to jump in some unexpected manner. Although scientists are confident that a frog does hear with its ears, this is more of a very well tested belief than a strictly proven fact.

Generalizations can never be proven true but they can easily be proven false. Even one conflicting fact will refute them. If our scientist were to train a frog to croak on command instead of having it jump, he could easily prove that a frog does not hear with its legs.*

In the real world, scientists are able to invent general rules which will explain all they see and which will predict the results of every experiment they perform for hundreds of years. Then, along comes an exception. The Michelson and Morley experiment, which will be examined in chapter 4, is such an exception. This is how science works; a generalization is never known to be true with absolute certainty.

If scientists are limited like this, it seems strange that they can perform useful work. Yet they certainly can accomplish great things. They discover cures for diseases, put men on the moon, invent terrible weapons, and do a great deal more. Although they are not always right, their system does seem to work for them most of the time.

Scientists are successful because they are able to sort their generalizations into different categories of certainty. Three categories which they use are "hypothesis," "theory," and "law."** These terms—and also the term "fact"—will be explained here, but keep in mind that there are no firm rules about how they are to be used. Different scientists tend to use them differently.

When a scientist climbs into a spacecraft and is launched into space, he puts his life on the line. Space launches are dangerous, but amazingly, most of them work as planned. Where his life is concerned, a scientist will trust only those

---

* Or at least he could prove that a frog did not hear *exclusively with its legs.*

** The level of confidence can also be expressed in mathematical terms. For example, 99.7% sure.

generalizations in which he has the most confidence. When a scientist's reputation is all that is at stake, he might be willing to "lighten up" a little. When he is privately discussing new ideas with other scientists, his wildest speculations are acceptable.

The lowest speculative level of certainty is labeled "hypothesis." A hypothesis is merely a first guess. A scientist who has never been outdoors in his entire life might hypothesize that all leaves are red. This, although false, could nevertheless be a perfectly good hypothesis—at least until an actual leaf was examined. If the examined leaf happened to be green, then the hypothesis would be refuted; it would no longer be valid.

The scientist might then hypothesize that all leaves are green. Now, when another green leaf is examined, the hypothesis will be supported rather than refuted. Of course a second green leaf does not prove the hypothesis to be a fact; it only tends to confirm it.

The next step up the chain of certainty is called "theory." The term "theory" is actually used to mean two slightly different things. One meaning of "theory" describes a hypothesis which has stood up under some experimental verification. Assume that our scientist has made his generalization (all leaves are green), has made predictions based on the rule (all of the leaves in a particular garden will therefore be green), and has verified that his predictions were correct (those leaves, when examined, did turn out to be green). At this point, he might say that it is his "theory" that all leaves are green. Although he still doesn't know for sure, he is more certain after checking all the leaves in a garden than he was after he had examined just one leaf.

Even after making this additional progress, if one single red leaf were ever found it would still refute the generalization that "all leaves are green." Our scientist would no longer have a valid theory or even a valid hypothesis. The generalization would be an error. Of course, the scientist could start over again with a different hypothesis. If he had found the red leaf during the month of August, for example, he might hypothesize that all leaves are green during the springtime.

At this point it is natural to ask how much experimental verification is required to promote a hypothesis to theory. There is no single answer to this question. Experiments are all different and so the decision is somewhat arbitrary. Different fields of science require different levels of experimental verification before the promotion is recognized, and this promotion is never formal. Physics typically requires the most verification—psychology perhaps the least.[2] The level is set purely as a practical matter depending on the difficulty of performing experiments and how precisely the results of the experiment can be interpreted. A physicist can be more certain in one afternoon about how a rock falls than a psychologist can be in a lifetime about how a human brain works. Psychologists are, as a practical rule, permitted to promote their generalizations with much less confirmation; consequently, their theories are either more cautiously worded or are more frequently incorrect.

A second meaning of the term "theory" describes *any* idea structure which can be used to explain some of the world's facts. This idea structure usually provides a reason *why*—for example, the reason all leaves ought to be green is that chlorophyll must be present for photosynthesis, and chlorophyll is green. Even a first hypothesis can also be a "theory" in this second sense. Further, even when the generalization attains the confidence level of scientific "law" (described below), it will still be a "theory" in this sense. The term "theoretical basis" is sometimes used to describe the reason why. For example, the theoretical basis for organic evolution is that mutations are random and that the fittest resulting individuals tend to be the ones which survive and reproduce.*

The final step in confidence is from "theory" to scientific "law." A law is a theory which has proved to be correct every single time it was tested by anyone, anywhere, for a very long period of time.[3] Physicists, for example, seldom promote a theory to the status of "law" without first testing it for many decades. Before this step is taken, all rival theories should be eliminated; a generalization is only regarded as a law when it is the only known way to explain the world's data (or at least the simplest of the known ways).

If our scientist had never been able to find a single leaf which was not green, and if he and many other scientists had been searching for one for many years, it might be proper to say that it was a scientific law that all leaves are green. Still, this would not make it a "fact" in the normal sense of the word. There would always be the chance that someone might discover a red leaf one day.

The finding of a single red leaf would refute a law that all leaves are green just as it would refute a theory or hypothesis. Our scientist's statement that "All leaves are green" would, as before, simply be an error. He would be forced to start over again with a new hypothesis (or a modified version of an old one).

The highest recognized category of certainty for generalizations is scientific "law." The status of "fact" is not scientifically attainable for any inferred generalization. The term "fact" is restricted to the observable data.[4] For example, it could be a "fact" that one particular leaf was green at one time.

---

*I believe that God was responsible for the design of every one of His creatures—that random processes played no significant part in this. I also believe that minor "evolutionary" change occurs within each of the kinds which God created. This is responsible for minor adjustments. Here random mutations and survival fitness are the primary guiding factors.

Because there are a lot of scientists at work sorting out each other's ideas, a great deal of progress has been made. Before a scientist's theories are even published, other experts in related fields are permitted to poke holes in them. Scientists take great delight in proving each other wrong; consequently, they keep each other in line. For this reason, it is very unlikely that you will ever read in a scientific journal that a frog hears with its legs, but this is still no guarantee that everything you read will be the truth. Scientists are human and humans sometimes make mistakes.

Seeking Truth

Although theologians sometimes fail to admit it, they are really in the same boat as the scientists. They have God's written Word, but they have no written directions telling them how to interpret it. In the final analysis, this means they encounter the same problems the scientists do. Theologians are human too.

For example, a theologian might say, "If the plain sense makes sense, look for no other sense." Although a literal interpretation of Scripture should always be the first choice, this poetic little rule (taken at "plain sense") goes right past good advice and tells us that if our first superficial reading makes sense to us then we should not even bother to look at more evidence to see if we might have made a mistake. This is not only bad advice, it also contradicts Scripture. As 1 Thessalonians 5:21 tells us, we must "test everything." A theologian who grounds his theories upon God's Word would need to modify this rule to something like "If the plain sense makes sense, test it anyway."

The young-earth teaching is, at least in part, the result of theologians forming dogmatic theories after examining the biblical evidence and paying insufficient attention to God's creation. This is almost as difficult as trying to understand God's plan of salvation using only the Old Testament. The information in the Old Testament is much less specific;

mistakes will invariably be made. Furthermore, once the wrong understanding has been reached, no amount of explaining away the additional facts of salvation found in the New Testament will ever make that first misunderstanding true. Only a discarding of the first error and the forming of a new theory using the combined data from both Testaments will bring a person to the truth.

The same principle applies to a mistake about the age of God's creation. Once the mistake has been made, no amount of explaining away the rest of the evidence will ever turn that error into the truth. It is necessary to start completely over again and study both God's Bible and His universe together as a single unit. It would be foolish not to pay close attention to any evidence that God's universe might directly supply concerning its own creation—nearly as foolish as ignoring God's written account.

Both the Bible and the universe must be interpreted in a manner which does not contradict *any* of the actual facts contained in the combined whole. When a conflict is found between our understanding of the Bible and our understanding of the universe, we must *not* look for errors in either the Bible or the universe; we must look for errors in *our understanding.* It is the intent of this book never to contradict a word in Scripture nor an observable fact of God's creation.

This method of seeking truth is not strictly scientific or theological. When it proves necessary, we will freely discard the sacred *methods* and *theories* of either side in favor of the other side's *facts. Be warned!* We humans are unaccustomed to this technique. It will bother both scientists and theologians.

Whoever you are, this book is likely to challenge some of your cherished beliefs. Unfortunately, having comfortable old ideas challenged can be emotionally difficult—and strong emotions can make clear thinking difficult. If you happen to be a theologian, it might become a challenge to separate God's Word from your interpretation of it. Likewise, you might find it easy to label the creation's physical evidence as "my opinions." Because of this, you will want to accuse me of bending Scripture to fit my opinions whenever I attempt to bend your opinions about Scripture to fit the scientific facts. Please be aware of this natural tendency and try to rightly divide between fact and theory.

Although this book confronts old *theories*, it will never contradict the *facts* found in either God's Scriptures or in His creation. However, even with both scientific evidence and Scripture as our guides, there is still room for us to make mistakes. History teaches that it is possible to be wrong even when scientific evidence and Scripture both seem to agree with a person's beliefs. Before Galileo, most scientists[5] believed that the earth was the stationary center of the solar system and that the sun orbited around it. Those who studied the Scriptures found them to be in agreement. In this case, both the scientists and the theologians were wrong! When Galileo began teaching the Copernican system—that the earth orbited the sun—he was attacked from both sides. Galileo was a Catholic and believed that his teaching was in agreement with the Word of God. Still, he was regarded as being both a heretic and a bad scientist. Here is what the Inquisition had to say about his teaching:

> The proposition that the Sun is in the centre of the world and does not move from its place is absurd and false philosophically and formally heretical, because it is expressly contrary to the Holy Scriptures.[6]

In case any readers still haven't got the word, the earth does orbit the sun—not the other way around. The idea that the sun travels around a stationary earth is not only very old-fashioned, it also happens to be wrong.* So how is it that the Inquisition could have come up with the idea that Galileo was contradicting the Scriptures? It seems that Galileo's critics

---

* Actually, modern cosmology provides a sort of defense for the Inquisition's position. According to the laws of relativity, any frame of reference can be taken as a stationary center of the universe. Of course this argument supports Galileo's position equally well.

were guilty of the same mistake which many of the present-day young-earth creationists have made. That is, they took the *plainest* reading of the Scriptures as the "true" one and disallowed any alternate interpretations. For example, Psalm 19:4-6 says, "In the heavens he has pitched a tent for the sun, which is like a bridegroom coming forth from his pavilion, like a champion rejoicing to run his course. It rises at one end of the heavens and makes its circuit to the other...." This verse and many others, such as "The sun rose" in Genesis 32:31, were probably taken by the Inquisition to mean that it was the sun moving across the sky, not the earth turning, which caused day and night. This would be the plainest reading of these verses (freely ignoring the obviously figurative parts). Still, it happens to be a wrong conclusion.

These scriptural references are of a type often called "observer true." They are what appears to be true to an earthbound observer. Even modern scientists will say things like "The sun is going down." This is not really a *false* statement; it is simply the way this thought is expressed in our language. The writers of the Bible must be allowed at least as much freedom in their use of language as we give ourselves.

In this example, even though scientific theories and theological interpretations seemed to agree, both were wrong. As is now known, Galileo was correct—even though he was unable to scientifically prove his case to his inquisitors.[7] If he had not repented of his "heresy," he might have been burned at the stake as was Bruno before him. Although a great scientist, Galileo was not a martyr. He compromised the truth in order to save the short remainder of his life.

Obviously, we must be very cautious. Even if our interpretation of Scripture is in complete agreement with what scientists happen to believe at present, both understandings might be in error at the same time. When the evidence proves that we have been in error, we must be ready and willing to admit it; we must be honest. If we are unable to face up to our mistakes in this life, it will be difficult for us to stand before God and give an account of ourselves (Romans 14:10-12). This is especially important if our mistakes happen to present stumbling blocks to our brothers (Romans 14:13).

Finally, seeking God's truth must come before other goals such as making peace or preserving unity. If we all come to the truth, then peace and unity will naturally follow, but if we pursue peace or unity instead, we are unlikely to reach the truth. Surprisingly, even the goal of avoiding compromise can lead to trouble. If our friend Joe erroneously believes that water freezes at 30 degrees Fahrenheit and another friend Moe believes it freezes at 50 degrees, Joe might accuse us of compromising with Moe when we say the correct freezing point is 32 degrees. The goal of avoiding compromise can lead us away from the truth as easily as toward it. What must never be compromised is the truth itself.

Conclusions

Science and theology are both fallible systems for seeking truth. God's Bible and His universe both supply unerring facts. Our own theories should be built upon the facts from both God's Bible and His creation. Even then, we must allow for the possibility that we might still make mistakes. Perhaps the most important lesson we should learn from this is humility.

3

The Present-Day
Stumbling Block

Woe to the world because of *its* stumbling blocks! For
it is inevitable that stumbling blocks come; but woe to
that man through whom the stumbling block comes!

— MATTHEW 18:7 NASB

The whole question concerning the age of the universe
hangs on the length of the six creative "days" in the first
chapter of Genesis. There the entire process of creation, from
the heavens right down to man, is described as a sequence of
six "days." In this chapter we will investigate some biblical
information concerning the length of those "days." More
specifically, we will consider those arguments presented in
support of the position that the "days" must be six consecutive
24-hour periods. Because nearly all scientists assure us that
the events described within those six "days" covered a span of
billions of years, we ought to examine the biblical information
very carefully.

Christians are often inclined to take the young-earth position simply because it appears to be the plainest reading of
the Bible. In the first chapter, we learned why we should be

more careful than this: Ancient writings, like Genesis, can be difficult to understand; the plainest reading may not necessarily be the correct one. God may actually have intended a meaning in Genesis which is different from the plain reading.

If the "days" in the first chapter of Genesis were longer than 24 hours, we might wonder why God chose wording which would tend to hide the truth from men of our present day. He certainly would have realized this would cause complications. Would God knowingly allow people to miss the truth? Clearly, before even the soundest of arguments for the old-earth interpretation can be taken seriously, this question needs to be answered.

Is it possible that God might have worded His truth in a way which would hide it from people? Is there any scriptural evidence of God hiding important things? As it turns out, there is. For example, in Isaiah 45:15 we are told, "Truly you are a God who hides himself, O God and Savior of Israel." Here we see that God hides himself. There are many places where the Bible tells us that God hides the truth. Consider the reason Jesus spoke in parables. There is no need to speculate about this because Jesus Himself explained the reason to His disciples in Matthew:

> The knowledge of the secrets of the kingdom of heaven has been given to you, but not to them. Whoever has will be given more, and he will have an abundance. Whoever does not have, even what he has will be taken from him. **This is why I speak to them in parables**:
>
> > "Though seeing, they do not see; though hearing, they do not hear or understand.
>
> In them is fulfilled the prophecy of Isaiah:
>
> > "'You will be ever hearing but never understanding; you will be ever seeing but never perceiving.

> For this people's heart has become calloused; they hardly hear with their ears, and **they have closed their eyes. Otherwise they might see with their eyes**, hear with their ears, understand with their hearts and turn, and I would heal them.'"

—MATTHEW 13:11-15, EMPHASIS ADDED

Here God intentionally hides the truth from His own chosen people. God's reason, it appears, is to allow them to make their own choices. Because God has not spoken plainly, those who do not want to see the truth can easily close their eyes. They do not have to understand God's message and turn to Him.

Although God never lies,* it seems He does not always present His truth in the plainest possible manner. God hides His messages in biblical parables and buries His truths deeply in the earth's crust. Although we may have to keep our eyes open and search diligently to discover the truth, we will never find a lie in either God's Bible or His universe.

There is an important difference between hiding the truth and outright deception. God will never lie. Following God's example, parents should not lie to their children, but it is often a good idea to hide things from them—especially potentially dangerous things. Other times, rewards are hidden which are intended to be found; an Easter egg hunt is an example of this. Parents who hide Easter eggs often hide them differently for children of different ages. Younger children may be given a head start.

Likewise, there are different spiritual abilities. The Jews had an advantage over the Gentiles in recognizing the Messiah. They were the ones who had studied the Scriptures which spelled out exactly what the Messiah must be like (Psalm 22). They had been warned of the exact time of His coming (Daniel 9:25,26). Paul refers to the advantages given them as being, "much in every way" (Romans 3:2). Yet Jesus

---

* Numbers 23:19; Hebrews 6:17,18; Titus 1:2

was a "stumbling block" for them (1 Corinthians 1:23). Jesus presented Himself to them in a form which they found too hard to accept. Was it because God deliberately hid the truth from them? Paul says that it *was*!

> What Israel sought so earnestly it did not obtain, but the elect did. The others were hardened, as it is written:
>
> "God gave them a spirit of stupor, eyes so that they could not see and ears so that they could not hear, to this very day."
>
> —Romans 11:7,8

Apparently this was deliberate.* God hides things from the wise and intelligent; but he reveals them to little children (Luke 10:21). This would be terribly unfair were it not for the fact that the wise and intelligent can find even hidden things if they are honestly looking for them. In Proverbs 25:2, Solomon tells us: "It is the glory of God to conceal a matter; to search out a matter is the glory of kings." It seems God has concealed things for the wise (like Solomon's "kings") to search out; children are given the extra help they need. On one hand, *anyone* who seeks will find (Matthew 7:7,8). God rewards those who earnestly seek Him (Hebrews 11:6); a lack of intelligence will not hinder a sincere seeker. On the other hand, if a person is not seeking God, his intelligence will not help him. The Bible tells us that God sometimes sets things up this way; it becomes possible for the less advantaged to find the truth while the more advantaged are hindered from merely blundering into it. The more we examine biblical stumbling blocks, the less unfair they appear.

Returning to Genesis, God certainly *could have* told us about the age of His creation in plainer or more detailed language. But if He did, would scientists have been able to close

---

* See also 2 Corinthians 3:14,15.

their eyes to the evidence? Seeing accurate technical information, which has only been discovered recently, on the very first page of the Bible would be difficult to ignore! It is more likely that God would give scientists a chance to make their own choices, like He did Israel. Because God has *not* spoken plainly, scientists who do not want to see the truth can easily close their eyes; they do not have to understand God's message and turn to Him.

This would also make Genesis more difficult for the rest of us to understand, but this didn't prevent God from using parables. After all, God is more interested in who has believed His Word and has received His Son Jesus as Savior than He is with who understands the time schedule of His creation.

In any case, we must allow that Genesis might be very difficult to understand—so difficult that it could confound even the wise or scientific. The extreme antiquity of the account could certainly accomplish this. We have good reason to be careful as we evaluate different interpretations of the Genesis "days"; we must look past any superficial meanings and make sure we have the *correct* understanding.

With this in mind, we will examine the following eight arguments. These have been proposed by young-earth creationists as reasons why the Genesis "days" *must* be understood as six consecutive 24-hour periods.*

Arguments for 24-hour days:

1) The 24-hour interpretation is the most literal reading of the text; God would have used alternate wording if He had intended the "age" interpretation.

2) Genesis 1:14 forces the 24-hour interpretation by using "yom" in a context which excludes the "age" possibility.

---

* Some additional arguments which merely allow for this possibility will be dealt with in the next chapter.

3) The use of the expression "evening and morning" limits the days to 24 hours.

4) The use of a number appended to the word "day" requires the 24-hour interpretation.

5) The 24-hour interpretation is forced by the reference to Genesis 1 in Exodus 20:9-11, where our workweek is explained.

6) The "age" interpretation must be wrong since it carries a consequence that death must have preceded sin and the fall.

7) According to Mark 10:6, Adam must have been created at the beginning of creation, not billions of years later.

8) The only reason for the "age" interpretation is to accommodate the evolutionists.

These are typical of arguments given in support of the young-earth position; they are intended to be representative of the best arguments. Their full text is provided in appendix 2 so anyone who is interested can examine these arguments in their original context.

Although this appears to be an impressive battery, each of these arguments contains at least one fatal flaw. This will be seen as they are examined one at a time. We must remember that these are all just theological *theories* designed by fallible men. Not one of them is actual Scripture. Theories can never be proven true, but each of these will be proved false as it is examined in detail.

Argument #1

The 24-hour interpretation is the most literal reading of the text; God would have used alternate wording if He had intended the "age" interpretation.

Rebuttal to Argument #1

Were it not for the complications we have been exploring, this would certainly seem like a good argument. Although "yom" can refer to an indefinite period of time, this is not obvious to an English reader today. But, as we have seen, this argument neglects some important information.

First, God sometimes hides truth from the wise and He might have done so here. Next, Genesis is an extremely ancient writing; it was not originally written in the "plain English" we see in our modern Bibles. Also, there are places in Genesis where the plainest reading is simply wrong. In Genesis 3:20, for example, the plainest reading tells us that Eve gave birth to animals as well as men: "Adam named his wife Eve, because she would become the mother of **all the living**" (emphasis added). Clearly "all the living" refers only to humans. Insisting on the very *plainest* reading would violate simple common sense in this case. For these reasons, the creation account in Genesis is likely to be difficult to understand.

Furthermore, insisting on the plainest or most literal reading might have caused trouble even if God had used a different word to describe the "days" of Genesis. "Yom" usually refers to a 24-hour period, but the next closest Hebrew word "olam" usually means "forever." Using "olam" would only have replaced one wrong "literal" reading with another.

This first argument fails. We obviously need to use more caution than it recommends. The decision about the length of the Genesis "days" will need to be made on some other basis than the "most literal" reading of the words God chose.

Argument #2

Genesis 1:14 forces the 24-hour interpretation by using "yom" in a context which excludes the "age" possibility.

Rebuttal to Argument #2

This argument says that since the word "days"* in verse 14 is used in a context which can only mean a sequence of 24-hour periods, other usages of the word "day" in the same passage must follow suit and also refer to 24-hour periods.**

The use of the same word in a closely related passage is a good general rule of interpretation, but this rule must not be applied carelessly. Because the word "day" is used many times in this passage, *all* of the usages should be considered to get the whole picture—not just one from verse 14.

In the first two chapters, where the "days" in question are found, the word "day" occurs fifteen times and the word "days" once. The single occurrence of the word "days" carries the 24-hour meaning. Of the remaining fifteen usages, nine refer to the days of creation themselves. No assumptions can be made about them because that would be "begging the question."*** Of the remaining six, the context forces the 12-hour daylight meaning four times and a greater-than-24-hour meaning twice.****

Because "day" is used so many different ways in the surrounding context, this argument cannot tell us the length of the creation "days." Argument #2 also fails. Obviously the use of the same word in the surrounding context is not an infallible guide to the meaning of that word.[1] Again, the decision about the length of the creative days must be made on some other basis.

Argument #3

The use of the Hebrew expression "evening and morning" limits the days to 24 hours.

---

*   "Days" is "yamim" in Hebrew which is simply the plural of "yom."

**   Actually, the only occurrence of "day" (singular) in verse 14 refers to the 12 daylight hours as opposed to night. Only the plural occurrence "days" refers to 24-hour periods.

***   "Begging the question," means assuming in advance a conclusion to a particular problem, then using that assumption as data to help determine the solution. This is a form of circular reasoning.

**** Genesis 2:4 uses "yom" (singular) in a context which is usually taken to refer back to several of the creative days. Genesis 2:17, as we have seen, is the "day" in which Adam died.

Rebuttal to Argument #3

This argument is presented as if it were a general rule of interpreting Scripture, but no reason is provided as to why it should be considered a valid one. Like the word "day," the Hebrew words for "evening" and "morning" ("ereb" and "boqer") both have usages which are not limited to 24-hour periods.

When we say in English that a convenience store is open "day and night," "A.M. and P.M.," or even "24 hours" we do not mean that it will close after a single 24-hour day has passed; what we mean is that it is open continuously, day after day. The same is often true of the Hebrew words for "evening" and "morning" where they occur together in God's Word.

In Exodus 18:13, for example, Moses is wearing himself out because he judges the people "morning till evening." When we read this passage, we understand from context that this means he is doing it day after day. This is why it was necessary for capable men to be appointed to serve as judges (verses 21,22) and to spare Moses. If the words "evening" and "morning" had really limited this event to a single 24-hour period, the appointments would have been unnecessary.

For a few more examples, in Exodus 27:21 Aaron and his sons are to keep the lamps burning before the Lord "evening till morning"; again we understand this to mean continually, day after day. This is also seen in Leviticus 24:3: "Aaron is to tend the lamps before the Lord from evening till morning, **continually**" (emphasis added). Job 4:20 speaks figuratively of men's "houses" of clay which are destroyed between "morning and evening." This process seems slow to men but not to God. Daniel 8:14 uses "evening" and "morning" singular[2] (translated "days" in the KJV and "evenings and mornings" in the NIV) to refer to a period of 2,300 days.

Rather than limiting a time period to 24 hours, God's Word shows us that the words "evening" and "morning" often imply a period which goes on indefinitely. Although there are exceptions (Numbers 9:21, for example, uses the phrase "evening till morning" in a 12-hour context), most usages appear to address a time period in excess of 24 hours. If readers would like to research this further, some other usages are 1 Samuel 17:16;* 1 Chronicles 16:40; 2 Chronicles 2:4, 31:3; Ezra 3:3; Psalm 55:17; and Daniel 8:26.

Obviously the expression "evening and morning" does not establish that the "days" of creation were 24 hours in length. Argument #3 fails to prove what it claims. Those who have suggested it do not appear to have checked very carefully if their argument was really the truth. It would seem that we still don't have a clear way to interpret the word "day." As before, the decision should be made on some other basis.

Argument #4

The use of a number appended to the word "day" requires the 24-hour interpretation.

Rebuttal to Argument #4

If it is *always* true that a biblical "day" with a number appended to it is 24 hours long, then the Genesis "days" must all be 24-hour periods. But if this generalization is not always true, then we will have to find another way to make this decision. In order to prove this generalization is false, we must find a number appended to the word "day" in a special scriptural context where we can be certain that the "day" in question lasted for more than 24 hours. Zechariah 14:7 contains the number "one" appended to "day" in a context which certainly refers to a daylight period of indefinite length:

> But it shall be **one day** which shall be known to the Lord, not day, nor night; but it shall come to pass, *that* at evening time it shall be light.
>
> —KJV, EMPHASIS ADDED

---

* Here the word for morning is "shakam."

This is a description of the new Jerusalem in which there is no night. The special context of this verse makes it difficult to misunderstand; the same prophetic event is described in detail in Revelation 22:5. In this verse, the one single "day" (period of daylight) is understood to last for a very long (indefinite) period of time. The phrase "one day" (used here), and the phrase "the first day" (used in Genesis 1:5), are both translated from the exact same Hebrew phrase "yom echad," literally "day one." Because of the special context of Zechariah 14:7, we can be certain that the "one day" is longer than 24 hours in length. The *theory* that a number used with the word "day" always forces the 24-hour understanding is simply false.

In Genesis 1:5 there are seven different Hebrew words which are sometimes offered as contextual evidence for the 24-hour interpretation—they are "day," "night," "evening," "morning," "light," "darkness," and the number "one" (translated "first"). Of these seven, five are present in Zechariah 14:7; only "morning" and "darkness" are missing. With regard to these seven words, this is the closest contextual match in the entire Bible; and it speaks of a day which is much longer than 24 hours. The next closest match, outside of Genesis 1, is Job 17:12 with only four of the seven words.*

It is also interesting to consider the "last" day referred to in the Bible. Although "last" is not strictly a number, it is certainly grammatically analogous to "first" and hence deserves consideration here. Isaiah 30:8 reads, " . . . that for the days to come it may be an everlasting witness."

The phrase "for the days to come" has been translated from two Hebrew words meaning "for the day" and "latter"[3]— or in other words, "for the last day." The Hebrew "day" (singular) was translated "days" because it is obvious from context that a long period of time was intended. The NASB translated "day" as "time" in this verse for the same reason. This should not surprise anyone.

---

* Job 17:12 will not help us sharpen our understanding of the meaning of words here. Job is merely accusing his adversaries of confusing day with night and darkness with light.

Argument #4 also fails. The formula of "a number appended to the word 'day'" does not require the 24-hour interpretation; parallel applications of the rule speak of long "days." God certainly has as much right to attach numbers to indefinite periods of time as He does to attach them to 24-hour periods. The numbers appended to the "days" in Genesis prove nothing at all about the length or meaning of those days. Again, the decision must be made on some other basis.

Argument #5

The 24-hour interpretation is forced by the reference to Genesis 1 in Exodus 20:9-11, where our workweek is explained.

Rebuttal to Argument #5

In Exodus 20:9-11, God gives the reason for our schedule of six days of work to one day of rest:

> Six days you shall labor and do all your work, but the seventh day is a Sabbath to the LORD your God. On it you shall not do any work, . . . For in six days the LORD made the heavens and the earth, the sea, and all that is in them, but he rested on the seventh day.

Because our workdays and Sabbath rests are 24-hour days and because they are modeled after God's, we are expected to conclude that God's days must have been 24-hour ones also. Before we make a decision, however, we must also examine other biblical information.

For example, God's Word warns us that many things in the Bible are merely shadows of greater heavenly truths—in fact, it specifically warns us that *Sabbath days* are such shadows. Paul tells us this in Colossians 2:16,17:

> Therefore do not let anyone judge you by what you eat or drink, or with regard to a religious festival, a New Moon celebration or a **Sabbath day**. These are a

shadow of the things that were to come; the reality, however, is found in Christ.

—EMPHASIS ADDED

A slightly different view of this can be seen in Hebrews 8:5:

They serve at a sanctuary that is a copy and shadow of what is in heaven.

It is never very safe to make absolute conclusions about the true length of an object by merely looking at its shadow. We can see from other Scripture that this warning applies directly to the length of workweeks. Leviticus 25:3,4 tells us:

For six years sow your fields, ... But in the seventh year the land is to have a sabbath of rest, ...

It is clear that this pattern of work and rest for our fields is also a shadow of God's workweek, but it does not follow that God's "days" were 365 days long. God's workweek has cast shadows of two different lengths—six days and six years; they cannot both be equal in length to God's. In fact, there is no reason either of them needs to be.

Before we presume to gauge the length of God's week based on our own human unit of measure, we really ought to reflect that God's week is *not* a shadow of ours but that ours is a shadow of His. Because it does not really follow from the work "week" of our fields that God's "days" were 365-day years, neither does it follow from our workweek that God's "days" were 24-hour periods.

Notice also what Hebrews says about Sabbaths:

For somewhere he has spoken about the seventh day in these words: "And on the seventh day God rested from all his work." And again in the passage above he says, "They shall never enter my rest." It still remains that some will enter **that rest,** ... Therefore God again set a certain day, calling it **Today,** when a long time later he spoke through David, as was said before:

"Today, if you hear his voice, do not harden your hearts."

For if Joshua had given them rest, God would not have spoken later about *another* day. There **remains**, then, a Sabbath-rest for the people of God; for anyone who enters **God's rest** also rests from his own work, just as God *did* from his.

—HEBREWS 4:4-10, EMPHASIS AND ITALICS ADDED

Here it sounds very much as if God's Sabbath rest is still in progress today and is the same rest that we are to enter into.* The italicized word is not present in the original Greek[4] of the New Testament and so verse 10 does not really identify God's rest as a past event. Context implies that "as God *is doing* from his" would be a more correct paraphrasing. It would seem that at least God's seventh day is longer than 24 hours.

Because Argument #5 is based on a mere shadow, it fails to force the 24-hour interpretation. In fact, as we have seen, there is even some scriptural indication that God's Sabbath day is still in progress. The final decision about the length of the creative days must not be based on this argument either.

Argument #6

The "age" interpretation must be wrong since it carries a consequence that death must have preceded sin and the fall.

Rebuttal to Argument #6

The "age" interpretation does disagree with some traditional beliefs concerning the fall. According to the fossil evidence, the dinosaurs became extinct more than 60 million years before man was created. This means they must have died

---

* The idea that God's seventh-day rest is still in progress fits with the rest of Scripture where this is mentioned. Jesus said, "My father is always at his work to this very day, and I, too, am working" (John 5:17). This was to justify healing an invalid man on the Sabbath. Notice here that Jesus' argument would make sense however one interprets the duration of God's Sabbath; in either case it is understood that God is working during His Sabbath.

before Adam's fall. Furthermore, there is scientific evidence that many creatures, from before the time of men, ate other animals.[5] The evidence says there *was* animal death before Adam.

Although this disagrees with a popular scriptural *theory*, it is not in disagreement with Scripture itself. Scripture gives no reason why animals couldn't have died before Adam's sin. Adam was told that he would die as a result of his own sin. Paul points out that men who lived between Adam and Moses also died as a result of Adam's sin; but nowhere does the Bible say that *animals* die as a consequence of human sin.[6] (Of course those particular animals which were sacrificed as a sin offering are excepted.)

In support of Argument #6, young-earth creationists often cite Romans 5:12:

> ...just as sin entered the world through one man, and death through sin, and in this way death came to **all men**, because all sinned—...
>
> —EMPHASIS ADDED

When young-earth creationists read that "death" entered through sin, they interpret this as "all death" even though this verse specifically names *all men* as its target. *Human* death certainly entered through Adam's sin but this verse doesn't specifically address animal or plant death. Even where the Bible actually uses the word "all" we must be careful; as we saw back in Argument #1, the statement that Eve would become the mother of *"all the living"* does not mean she would become the mother of animals. We certainly should not insist on adding an "all" to God's Word. Because Paul specifically said death came to "all men," it is unreasonable to insist that he intended more than that.

Presumably, anyone who believes that animals did not die before Adam sinned must believe that up until that time carnivores ate plants in the same manner that "the lion will eat straw like the ox,"[7] during the millennium (Isaiah 11:7).

Even so, there must have been some form of death before Adam's fall. At the very least some parts of plants must have "died" to feed those animals. It is therefore plain that at least some form of plant death was in the world before Adam sinned.[8] It follows that when Paul said that death entered through sin, he could not possibly have meant *all* death.

In fact, there was even a *man* who lived and died after Adam yet was not under the curse of sin and death at all; Jesus was that exception. Consider what it was about Him that made Him acceptable as a sacrifice for our sins when no other human would do. The answer is, of course, that He was not guilty of sin; neither was He under its curse (Hebrews 4:15; 1 John 3:5). Only a man who had no sin, original or personal, would be properly qualified.

Now, if "all men" inherited Adam's original fallen nature, how is it that Jesus escaped this curse? Even those men who lived between Adam and Moses—those who had broken no specific law themselves (the law not having been given yet)—were under the curse of sin and owed the same price which Adam had to pay! None of them broke any specific written law, yet they all died. Why was Jesus different? Why was His death a sacrifice and not merely payment due?

One possibility stems from the fact that Jesus had no human father even though He did have a human mother. According to this theory, we somehow inherit original sin through our father's bloodline.[9] Another possibility is that God miraculously intervened and thus severed the connection to Adam's sin. Were it not for some such explanation, Jesus would have inherited Adam's original sin and could not have been "without sin" as the Bible establishes that He was. This seems to be why Adam's sin nature, and its inevitable consequence, was not passed on to Jesus as it was to everyone else; one way or another, Jesus was not entirely connected to Adam's lineage.

Now what about animals? Is there any possible way that they could have inherited Adam's sin nature? Of course not!

They are not Adam's descendants in any sense whatsoever. Therefore, they cannot be included with us in our fallen state. This is probably why they could be used for the Old Testament sacrifices; they were innocent.

Apparently, present-day animals are not under the curse of Adam's sin, yet they still die physically. It follows that animal death is not a result of Adam's sin. Animals would be dying even if Adam had not sinned. Ancient animals, which preceded Adam's fall, would also have died. This difference between Adam and the animals—that he might not have died while they would have in any case—was probably because Adam was created in the image of God (Genesis 1:27) while the animals were not.

So Argument #6, like Arguments #1 through #5, also fails to throw the case in favor of the 24-hour interpretation. Although the old-earth creationist's position carries the consequence that animal death must have preceded Adam's sin, this argument does not eliminate the old-earth position as a possibility. There really is no biblical reason why animals could not have died before Adam's fall. Once again, the decision must be made on some other basis.

Argument #7

According to Mark 10:6, Adam must have been created at the beginning of creation, not billions of years later.

Rebuttal to Argument #7

Adam was created on the sixth day of creation, not the first. This was not the beginning of creation no matter how long or short the creation days were. So why did Jesus say Adam was created at the beginning of the creation? What Jesus intended can be seen from the surrounding context and a closer look at the different possible meanings of the Greek word "ktisis," translated "creation" here.

> "It was because your hearts were hard that Moses wrote you this law," Jesus replied. "But at the beginning of **creation** God 'made them male and female.' 'For this reason a man will leave his father and mother and be united to his wife, and the two will become one flesh.' So they are no longer two, but one. Therefore what God has joined together, let man not separate."
>
> —MARK 10:5-9, EMPHASIS ADDED

Context shows us that Jesus is addressing the true meaning of the institution of marriage here. Although the Greek word "ktisis" usually means "the act of creation" or "the thing created," it can also refer to an "institution" or "ordinance"[10] as it does in 1 Peter 2:13: "Submit yourselves for the Lord's sake to every **authority instituted** among men..." (emphasis added). Here the two words "authority" and "instituted" are translated from the single Greek word "ktisis." Clearly what Jesus meant in Mark 10:6 is that from the beginning of the institution of marriage (no earlier than the sixth day) marriage was not intended to end in divorce.

Argument #7 also fails to prove the earth is young. In fact Mark 10:6 does not address the creation of the heavens and earth at all. Again we will need to find a different reason if we are to conclude the earth must be young.

Argument #8

The only reason for the "age" interpretation is to accommodate the evolutionists.

Rebuttal to Argument #8

I am an old-earth creationist, *not* an evolutionist. I have no desire to accommodate any errors—not even those of my fellow creationists. Argument #7 is not applicable in this case; and in any case, decisions should always be founded on the actual evidence—not on the biases or motives (real or imagined) of the various individuals who happen to hold the different positions.

This argument also encounters a difficulty with history. The scientific understanding that the earth is old came many years *before* Darwin's theory.[11] Therefore, it could not possibly have been an attempt to accommodate evolution in any way whatsoever.

How Long Were the Days of Genesis?

Each of the arguments for the 24-hour-day position failed when examined. In some cases, the scriptural evidence even suggested that the "days" were longer than 24 hours. There seem to be *no* valid scriptural arguments that the "days" of Genesis were consecutive 24-hour periods. If any exist, I certainly have not seen them. But there *is* evidence that those days were *not* consecutive 24-hour periods.

The Bible is truth, but God has written other truth as well. The universe is also God's work. The very same God who created the Bible also created the physical universe. *God does not lie—ever.* The Bible is quite clear about that.* He did not lie during the thousands of years when He was "writing" the Bible. He did not lie as He "wrote" the universe either. In case there is any doubt, we are told in the Bible that we see truth when we study God's universe:

> The heavens declare the glory of God; the skies proclaim the work of his hands. Day after day they pour forth speech; night after night they display knowledge.
>
> —Psalm 19:1,2

The Bible even tells us we can learn spiritual truth from God's creation:

> God's invisible qualities—his eternal power and divine nature—have been clearly seen, being understood from what has been made . . .
>
> —Romans 1:20

---

* Numbers 23:19; Hebrews 6:17,18; Titus 1:2

The Bible is God's Word and should be taken to mean exactly what it says—literally! How should the universe be read? It has the same Author. There is certainly no reason to assume that it should be taken differently than the Bible; God's universe deserves the same *literal* reading.

It is difficult to interpret the heavens and the earth correctly. Throughout history men have made many mistakes trying. This does not mean the universe itself cannot be trusted as a source of truth. As is well known, men have made just as many mistakes trying to interpret the Bible, yet the Bible itself can certainly be trusted! In either case, the true reading will not always be the "plainest," but there will be no lies included in the actual "text."

The hard evidence for a very old earth is real. This will become clear in the following chapters as some of the most misunderstood aspects of God's other "book"—the universe—are explored.

There will be stumbling blocks. Jesus said in Matthew 18:7 that this was inevitable. However, our responsibility as Christians is to make sure that we do not put them there; there will be "woe" to those who do! The "days" of Genesis 1 appear to present such stumbling blocks. It is most important that we are not responsible for magnifying these obstacles when we talk to non-Christians. We must not make our preaching more foolish than it absolutely needs to be (1 Corinthians 1:18-23). There is already enough hindrance in the world to keep people with scientific understanding from finding their way to Christ.

4

A Shadow
of Eternity

The heavens declare the glory of God; the skies pro-
claim the work of his hands. Day after day they pour
forth speech; night after night they display knowledge.

— PSALM 19:1,2

The universe was only created once. There were not two separate creations—one for the information in the first chapter of Genesis and another for the information seen through telescopes. It follows that there should be no contradictions between the two accounts.

God's universe demands a literal reading just like His Bible does. God's Word, in Psalm 19:1,2 (quoted above), explains that His creation "displays knowledge." Ironically, those Christians who are most insistent that we take the plainest meaning of every word in the Bible will go to great lengths to sidestep a literal reading of God's heavens. They are correct that God's Bible speaks the truth, but so do His heavens. God's Word ought to be trusted without disregarding the scientific reading of His creation. What is needed is a proper regard for both.

God's invisible qualities, such as His unfathomable timelessness, are written all over His heavens. As explained in previous chapters, the Bible even suggests God's heavens will reflect His eternal nature:

> God's invisible qualities—his **eternal** power and divine nature—have been clearly seen, being understood from what has been made . . .
>
> —ROMANS 1:20, EMPHASIS ADDED

When atheistic scientists read the heavens, they see an agelessness about them even when they fail to see something as obvious as the creation's need for a Creator. When young-earth creationists read the heavens they appear almost as blind as the atheistic scientists; they seem to be blinded to the incomprehensible age of the creation. It would seem that, of all people, it should be the Christians who would be able to see a "shadow" of God's eternal nature proclaimed in the heavens.

The universe is very old. Exactly how old is not known. Present estimates run in the 10–20-billion-year range, but even the scientists have not settled on an exact age. Only God really knows. Here it will be demonstrated that the universe is much older than the 24-hour interpretation of Genesis allows for. One of the simplest proofs is a consequence of the size of the universe and the speed of light.

The mathematics required to calculate how long it must take for something to move from point "A" to point "B" can be very simple. If we have an old car which will not go faster than 60 miles per hour, and if we must drive it a distance of 120 miles, then we know we cannot possibly make the trip in less than 2 hours. This is because 120 divided by 60 is 2; the distance divided by the velocity gives the time ($d/v=t$). If we want to make certain we know the time (t) correctly, we only need make certain that we know the distance (d) and the velocity (v). To figure out how much time it takes for light to get to us from distant stars, we need to know how far away those stars are and how fast light travels.

Distance / Velocity = Time

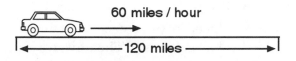

60 miles / hour

120 miles

120 miles / 60 miles/hour = 2 hours

If there is anything about the heavens that both creationists and evolutionists agree upon, it is that they are extremely large. We all have some concept of how large the earth must be, but it is difficult to fathom the 238,854-mile distance to the moon.[1] When we look at the moon at night, it is very hard to imagine that it is 2,160 miles in diameter and so very far away. Still, relatively speaking, the moon is not far away. The closest planets, Mars and Venus, never come nearly as close. The sun is a staggering 92,900,000 miles away from us. This is just as well; every second it unleashes trillions of times as much energy as the Hiroshima bomb. Even at our tremendous distance, a person can still get "burned by the sun."

The sun is very far from us, but the sun, the moon, the earth, and all the other planets sit together in a little group all alone by themselves in a giant sea of empty space. The stars are not even close to them. In fact, the entire 92,900,000 miles between the earth and the sun would become insignificant if we were to view our solar system from even the closest star; instead of a bright sun, we would see a little star; and no telescope ever made could pick out the earth. But if we were to go to the closest galaxy* outside our own, and from there view

---

* A galaxy is a cluster of millions or even billions of stars.

our own sun, together with a few billion of its closest neighboring stars,* they would be completely invisible without a telescope; and with a telescope they would appear as a dim little smudge against the black night sky. What's more, individual galaxies are virtually lost in the sea of the universe's superclusters. (Superclusters are large clusters made up of smaller clusters—which, in turn, each contain hundreds or thousands of individual galaxies.)[2] The universe is even larger than a supercluster. How much larger? Like its age, no one has yet figured out exactly how large the universe really is (except God who measures the heavens with His hand—Isaiah 40:12, 48:13).

The mere fact that distant stars can be seen proves that they were there a very long time ago. Light travels very rapidly—186,282 miles in a single second—but even at that speed, light must travel for more than two million years to reach us from even our closest neighboring spiral galaxy,[3] which is located in the constellation Andromeda and identified simply as "M31."[4] M31 is *that* far away from us!

If M31 were younger than two million years, light from it would not have had time to reach us; this means we would not even know there was an M31 galaxy. The light would still be in space somewhere between it and us—still rushing toward us. But the light has already arrived here from M31 and we *do* see it. So how old is M31? Anyone who suggests that it is less than two million years old is simply disregarding the evidence. The only *literal* reading of God's universe is that we see M31 because light has traveled from it to us, and that takes time!

M31 is far away, but compared to other things in God's universe, it is relatively close. Light from much more distant objects shows that the universe is older still; light takes more than 300 million years to reach us from the Coma-A1367

---

* This would include every star you have ever seen on a very dark night, and billions more besides.

supercluster[5] and many billions of years to reach us from the most distant quasars.[6]

In spite of this scientific evidence, there are still a great many creationists who hold that God created the universe about 10,000 years ago. The three following explanations are usually offered in defense of this position.

Explanations for Visible Starlight in a Young Universe

1) The stars are actually very close to us and are very small.

2) Light traveled faster in the past than it does today.

3) God created light in transit between the stars and us.

Explanation #1 & Rebuttal

The Stars Are Actually Very Close to Us and Are Very Small

When this explanation is even mentioned at all, it is not usually taken seriously. It is normally included merely as a logical possibility, but one which is not considered to be very likely.[7] After all, the astronomers were right about the distances to the Moon, Venus, Mercury, Mars, Jupiter, Saturn, Uranus, and Neptune. We know this because we've sent spacecraft to them. Why should astronomers suddenly be wrong—and so very wrong—only when they start to measure the distances to the stars?

The M31 galaxy will make a good enough example to refute explanation #1, even though there are other objects in the universe which are thousands of times farther away from us than it is. If M31 were close enough to be seen in a 10,000-year-old universe, then it would have to be within 10,000 light-years of planet Earth. (A light-year is not a unit of time but the *distance* light travels in a year.)* This means it would be 200 times closer to us than the astronomers say. Even this assumption would mean that M31 had been invisible for the first

---

* A light-year is about six trillion miles.

10,000 years of the universe's existence, and anything more distant than it would still be invisible for ages yet to come.

Of course, if a star is closer it will also appear brighter to an observer here on earth. According to the inverse square law of light intensity,[8] a star which is 200 times closer should appear 40,000 times brighter. But the stars in the M31 galaxy do not appear to be unexpectedly bright. This means that if they are 200 times closer than expected, they must also be 40,000 times dimmer than expected.

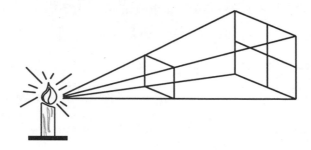

When an object is twice as far away, the same amount of light must cover four times the area. The area which the light must cover increases as the square of the distance.

A particular class of stars called Cepheid variables proves that stars in M31 are not dimmer than expected. These stars pulse at a rate which is linked to their absolute brightness. By merely watching their pulse rates, astronomers can know how bright these stars actually are. For this reason, it is clear that the Cepheid variable stars in the M31 galaxy are not dimmer and closer than astronomers say.[9]

Explanation #2 & Rebuttal

Light Traveled Faster in the Past Than it Does Today

Perhaps the best exposition of this idea has been done by Trevor Norman and Barry Setterfield.[10] Their explanation not only attempts to explain how distant stars can be seen, it also attempts to explain a few other supposedly related phenomena such as radioactive dating. Although this explanation also fails as a viable alternative to an old universe, it is still quite interesting. There is much to be learned about scientific inquiry from studying it closely.

In its outward appearance, this theory is supported by actual measurements which have been made of the speed of light over the past few hundred years. A curve has been fit reasonably well through these measurements—one which, when greatly extrapolated, indicates that the speed of light was extremely fast about 6,000 years ago[11]—fast enough to allow for the most distant stars to be visible in a young universe.

The claim is that the speed of light has been decreasing with time. Because the speed of light in a vacuum and in the absence of a strong gravitational field is so perfectly constant no matter how or where it is measured, Norman and Setterfield have added the restriction that the speed of light is the same everywhere in the universe at any given instant; they claim it varies everywhere at the same rate.[12] This is an attempt to reconcile this theory with Einstein's theory of relativity. What relativity has to say about this will be considered later, but first the data will be examined.

Ever since man realized that light did not travel instantaneously from one place to another, he has been trying to measure its speed. The first attempts were more crude than modern ones because of the limitations imposed by the available equipment, but as instrumentation improved, so did the measurements. At present the figure is known quite precisely to be 299,792,458 meters per second (to within some fraction of a meter), and measurements of centuries past (using very old-fashioned pendulum clocks) differed by only a fraction of a percent. The chart on pages 64 and 65 reports some of the historic measurements.

As can be seen from the graphical representation of this data (the top graph on page 66), if light changed speed at all

The Norman/Setterfield Speed of Light Data[13]

Date	Measured Value	Estimated Error	(Real Error)
1740	300,650,000	?	860,000
1783	300,460,000	160,000	670,000
1843	300,020,000	160,000	230,000
1861	300,050,000	?	260,000
1874	299,990,000	200,000	200,000
1874	299,900,000	200,000	110,000
1876	299,921,000	13,000	130,000
1879	299,910,000	50,000	120,000
1882	299,860,000	30,000	70,000
1882	299,853,000	60,000	60,000
1883	299,850,000	90,000	60,000
1900	299,900,000	80,000	110,000
1902	299,860,000	80,000	70,000
1902	299,901,000	84,000	110,000
1906	299,803,000	30,000	10,500
1923	299,795,000	30,000	2,500
1924	299,802,000	30,000	9,500
1926	299,798,000	15,000	5,500
1928	299,786,000	10,000	-6,500
1932	299,774,000	10,000	- 18,500
1936	299,771,000	10,000	- 21,500
1937	299,771,000	10,000	- 21,500
1940	299,776,000	10,000	- 16,500
1947	299,798,000	3,000	5,500
1947	299,792,000	3,000	- 460
1949	299,792,400	2,400	- 60
1949	299,796,000	2,000	3,500
1950	299,792,500	1,000	40

Date	Measured Value	Estimated Error	(Real Error)
1950	299,794,300	1,200	1,840
1950	299,793,100	260	640
1951	299,793,100	400	640
1951	299,794,200	1400	1740
1951	299,792,600	700	140
1953	299,792,850	160	390
1954	299,792,750	300	290
1954	299,795,100	3,100	2,640
1955	299,792,400	400	- 60
1955	299,792,000	6,000	- 460
1956	299,792,900	2,000	440
1956	299,792,700	2,000	240
1956	299,791,900	2,000	- 560
1956	299,792,400	110	-60
1956	299,792,200	130	- 260
1957	299,792,600	1,200	140
1958	299,792,500	100	40
1960	299,792,600	60	140
1966	299,792,440	200	- 20
1967	299,792,560	110	100
1967	299,792,500	50	40
1972	299,792,462	18	3?
1972	299,792,460	6	1?
1973	299,792,457.4	1.1	- 1?
1973	299,792,458	2	?
1974	299,792,459	0.8	?
1978	299,792,458.8	0.2	?
1979	299,792,458.1	1.9	?
1983	299,792,458.6	0.3	?

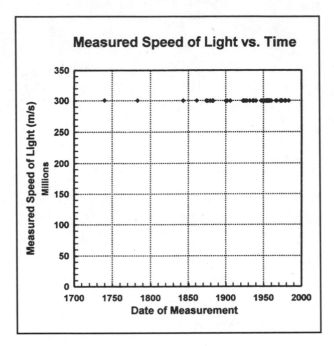

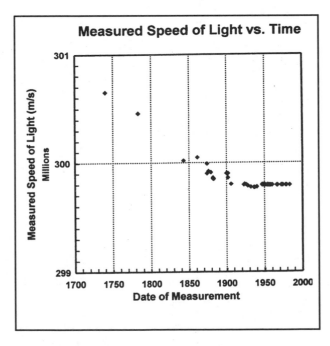

over the last 200 years, it certainly didn't change speed very much. The points make an almost perfectly level straight line.

In order to see the small amount of difference between the various measurements, the same data has been plotted with a greatly exaggerated vertical scale. On the bottom graph on page 66, the full scale represents less than 1 percent variation, and the zero point would be about 25 feet below the bottom of the page.

In the bottom graph on page 66 we can begin to see a decreasing trend in various light speed measurements over the last few hundred years, but this does not necessarily mean that the speed of light was really changing. There is a much simpler explanation: After the first few rough measurements were made, it appears that other scientists tended to be influenced by these early measurements. As a consequence, the accepted value approached the correct value more or less from one side,[14] instead of bouncing back and forth randomly between too fast and too slow quite as much as one might have expected if measuring error were truly random. Measuring error is seldom random. Scientists are people and people have expectations. The direction of experimental error is almost invariably influenced by these expectations. Even the best scientists are slightly inclined to discover what they expect to discover instead of what is really the truth.

It will be easy for us to understand how naturally scientists can fall into this trap and how the correcting process works; all we need to do is to pretend for a moment that we are scientists who are trying to measure the speed of light.

First we read that another scientist has measured the speed of light and found it to be 300,400,000 meters per second (m/s). We try it ourselves and get 299,700,000 m/s. We were close but we wonder why we weren't closer. So we try again, still using the same equipment; this time we get 299,900,000 m/s. This looks "better" to us though in fact it is slightly less accurate. We make many more measurements, "improving" our technique each time, but we rate our success largely on how close we come to 300,400,000 m/s; we have no other criteria to go by. Finally, we have "perfected" our technique and we are consistently measuring about 299,900,000 m/s; so we report our results.

We are almost certainly proud of our own ability and are quite willing to claim that the reason why our measurement differs from the earlier one is that ours is more accurate, but notice that we have still allowed it to influence our result slightly.

Eventually, better equipment comes along and the experiment is repeated with less error, but the scientists who repeat the experiment are also inclined to read the remaining error in favor of the traditional measurements. Each scientist in the chain is inclined to interpret the error in his instruments in favor of what the rest of the scientific community has found to be true before him. As time continues and instruments improve, scientists are forced farther away from the first mistake and converge upon the actual fact.

Like everyone, Norman and Setterfield certainly had their own expectations. As young-earth creationists, they presumably expected to discover that light used to travel faster in the past than it does now—enough so that light from the most distant stars could reach the earth within thousands of years. As they examined historic measurements of the speed of light, what they "saw" was that light has been slowing down ever since people started measuring it. Nearly all other scientists, in keeping with their expectations, "see" that the oldest measurements happened to be off and that subsequent measurements gradually corrected the measured speed down to the true value.

Norman and Setterfield selected a complicated mathematical curve which not only fit the historic data reasonably well but which also indicated that light from the most distant stars took something on the order of 6,000 years to reach us. A parabola (the very simplest mathematical curved line) would have fit their data as well or better, but it would not

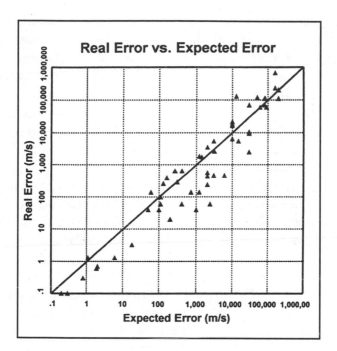

have borne out their expectation that the speed of light was many millions of times greater 6,000 years ago.[15]

When a scientist publishes his measurements, he usually reports an estimate of how much error they are likely to contain. Interestingly, most of the data points stray from the presently accepted value for light speed by about the amount of the estimated error. This can be seen in the graph above which compares the real error for each measurement with the error which each scientist expected his measurement to contain. The diagonal line shows where the points would be if the actual error was always exactly equal to the expected error. Points which are above this line correspond to measurements which contained more error than was expected; points below the line contained less. (Both of the scales are logarithmic so the wide range of errors can all be seen on the same graph.)

As this graph demonstrates, the real error is always within reasonable limits of what it ought to have been if light never changed speed. There is certainly no obvious trend to the contrary. This supports the hypothesis that the apparent change in light speed results from the reduction of measuring error with time. It also tends to confirm the suspicion that scientists sometimes interpret their data to agree with what they believe to be true.

Norman and Setterfield also claim that the rate of radioactive decay must change as the speed of light changes.[16] They predict radiocarbon dates for 4,000-year-old wood will appear much older—by about 34 million years. As will be shown in the next chapter, carbon-14 dates for 4,000-year-old wood turn out to be about 500 years *too young*. This observed *fact* refutes the Norman-Setterfield *theory* of light speed decay.

Although the Norman-Setterfield theory fails to stand up to close inspection, this does not prove that light from distant stars couldn't have reached us in mere thousands of years. Light still might have changed speed sometime in the past, even if there is no modern or historic data which confirms it. Light might have changed speed even if radioactive-dating evidence doesn't confirm it. The real adversary of changing light speed—Einstein's theory of relativity—will be addressed next.

Einstein's Theory of Relativity

Although popularly called the "theory" of relativity, Einstein's explanation has been experimentally tested for many years and has always done a good job of predicting the results of experiments. This gives relativity the status of scientific "law."*

In order to understand what relativity has to say about changing light speed, we need to know a little bit about relativity itself. This information will be presented as simply as

---

* This is true for the special theory at least. It is anticipated that the general theory of relativity will eventually need modification to harmonize it with quantum mechanics.

possible. Although relativity can be a brainteaser, I think you will find it quite interesting. The ideas behind relativity are not really very complicated; they are just very strange.

According to relativity, there is no preferred frame of reference. In other words, there is no place we can be, nor any speed at which we can be moving, that is more "true" in any sense than any other place or speed would be. In particular, it is impossible to ever know if we are moving very rapidly or are completely stopped. The laws of physics work just as well for a man in a high-speed train as they do for one who is standing still. If the man in the train throws a ball straight up, it will come back down into his hand instead of hitting the back wall of the car in which he is riding. This is still true even if the man in the train thinks he is standing still. After all, the earth is a giant moving "spaceship" which is traveling very rapidly around the sun, yet all of the laws of physics work for us as we move, even though we regard ourselves as being stationary.

The moving train example is an oversimplified one. It is easily explained, even without relativity. Not all things can be explained without it, however. This is why the laws of relativity were needed. How Albert Einstein came to the conclusion that there is no preferred frame of reference is not only an interesting story, it may also help us understand what relativity is about.

It all started back in the 1800s with the Nobel-prize-winning scientist, A. A. Michelson. Michelson had invented a new measuring apparatus with which he hoped to accurately measure the velocity of "spaceship Earth." This attempt is known as the Michelson-Morley experiment.

It was known that the earth makes one revolution on its axis daily. Because the earth is nearly 8,000 miles in diameter, this means that a man standing at the equator is being carried along by the turning earth at a speed slightly over 1,000 miles per hour.[17] Furthermore, the earth goes around the sun (total circular distance about 584,000,000 miles) once in a year. This means that the earth is zipping around the sun at more than

66,500 miles per hour. (And you are riding on it!) But how fast might the sun be moving through the galaxy or the galaxy through the universe? This is what Michelson wanted to measure.

Loosely speaking, Michelson's apparatus measured the speed of light as it passed the earth in one direction and very accurately compared it to the speed of light passing the earth in another direction. Because the earth was moving, it seemed to him that light should pass it at different speeds in different directions. As we have just seen, the earth is traveling at a pretty fast clip. The amazing result of the experiment was that no matter which way Michelson turned his apparatus, nor how carefully he made his measurement, he found that the apparent speed of passing light was always *exactly* the same— not *almost* the same; there was no observable difference at all!

Putting this into a common setting will reveal how absurd this measurement was. It was as if we were in a slowly moving car and we were watching faster cars on the same street which were passing us in both directions. Further, assume that all of those other cars were traveling at exactly the same speed, just like light does. We should expect cars which were overtaking us to pass us more slowly than those which were coming the opposite direction. What Michelson discovered was like saying that the cars were passing us at exactly the same rate in both directions;[18] it was as if we were completely stopped. This was not at all what Michelson was expecting to discover! He knew that the earth was moving many thousands of miles per hour through the universe. Occasionally scientists discover things which they are not expecting—but only when the evidence demands it.

The scientific community had a very hard time accepting this (just like you might now be having). Michelson was given lots of money to reconstruct his apparatus, and he rebuilt it using the best available techniques and equipment. This time his apparatus was built as solidly as a battleship. The experiment was repeated and, to the chagrin of the world, the results were exactly the same. The earth did not appear to be moving at all! Either the earth was the stationary center of the universe and the sun circled it, or new laws of physics were needed. Albert Einstein was able to figure out what had happened with Michelson's experiment; he provided the necessary new laws of physics to explain it.

Scientists found themselves in a position very much like the man on the train who could not tell from throwing his ball up into the air that he was moving—only their position was even worse; it was as if looking out the window wouldn't help either. According to the laws of relativity, the speed of light was always constant no matter how it was measured.[19] Instead, other things like the very rate of time itself would change. When Einstein came to this realization and provided the proper equations, Michelson's experiment made sense.

Apparently the rate of time actually does change! As it turns out, speed, acceleration, and gravity all affect it.[20] As incredible as this sounds, subsequent experiments confirmed Einstein's seemingly wild claim. Elapsed time for very high speed subatomic particles can be shown to be quite different than that for a stationary observer.[21] Small changes in the rate of time can even be detected using very accurate clocks carried on supersonic aircraft.[22] What time it is depends partly on where you are and how fast you are moving!

If one of a pair of identical twins were to be sent off into space for 50 years, traveling at speeds approaching the speed of light, something very strange would become apparent when the twins were reunited at the end of the journey. The earthbound twin would, naturally, find himself to be 50 years older than he had been, but the space traveler would have aged much less.[23] He could have aged as little as a year or less during his travels—depending on how fast he had been going. His spaceship was simply in something like what a science fiction writer might call a "time warp." That's the way the real universe is; time passes at different rates under different conditions.

As previously mentioned, Norman and Setterfield's theory requires that the speed of light changes at the same rate everywhere in the universe, so it is always the same everywhere at any given instant. The problem with this is that ideas like "at the same time" lose meaning when time advances at different rates under different conditions. There is just no way to know whose clock to use.

In fact, it turns out that there is no way at all to synchronize two widely separated clocks so that everyone will agree that they are in fact synchronized. "Now" here is not necessarily also "now" in another place.[24] Two clocks which are close together (like on the same planet) can be synchronized fairly well, but as they are moved farther apart the situation becomes hopeless. If clock "A" were placed on earth and clock "B" somewhere in the M31 galaxy, the attempt to synchronize would be futile. Some observers would see clock "A" rust into powder before a shiny new clock "B" was even placed into position. Others would see "B" turn to powder before a shiny new "A" was positioned. This confusion would still be there even after corrections were made for the time it took the light to reach the different observers.[25]

God's View of Time

Now to put this all together: It is known from measurements that the speed of light, in empty space, is the same everywhere right now. It is also known from relativity that our "now" is the same as "then" for some other observer. This means the speed of light, for some other observer, must also have been the same everywhere "then." It follows that the speed of light, again in empty space, must always be the same everywhere, and for all time, because a chain of "thens" and "nows" can be linked together from different frames of reference to tie all time together.[26]

In fact, according to Einstein's equations, time stands still for light in transit.[27] While billions of years might be passing for observers on planets, a photon (which is the smallest possible "particle" of light) will make its flight from a distant star in a literal instant of its own time. It is as if light, like God, is not subject to what men call time. A traveling photon reveals the same mystery that Jesus did in His statement, "Before Abraham was born, I am!" (John 8:58).

All of this may sound incredible, but this *is* the way the universe is made. No promise was made that the universe would be easy to understand, only that it would speak the truth. Remember, it's like its Creator; He is not easy to fathom either! God made the universe with a very complex relationship to time. The universe speaks of *His* invisible attributes, not ours. To Him, a thousand years *really* is as one day and vice versa (2 Peter 3:8). To us, a thousand years is a long, long time. As we study God's creation we should expect to see many more similarities between creation and Creator.

God uses His creation in many ways to teach us about Himself. He often teaches us spiritual truth through metaphors which, although they are mere shadows of spiritual truth, have been chosen from nature so carefully that their *physical* characteristics reflect in great detail the *spiritual* truths to which they relate. (Or, possibly, the physical realities may have been created with the desired spiritual reflection in mind.) For example, God sometimes calls us "sheep." We find that we can learn more about ourselves than we even care to know by studying real sheep in detail. In the words of a modern-day shepherd:

> It is no mere whim on God's part to call us sheep. Our behavior patterns and life habits are so much like that of sheep it is well nigh embarrassing.
>
> —A SHEPHERD LOOKS AT PSALM 23 [28]

Now that we understand that light's speed does not change,[29] we are in a better position to appreciate God's use of "light" as a metaphor. Truth and righteousness do not change from century to century but are forever the same. It appears that Jesus, who is the same yesterday, today, and forever

(Hebrews 13:8), and who could even say, "Before Abraham was born, I am!" (John 8:58) was speaking more graphically than many realize when He called Himself the "light" of the world (John 8:12).

Light cannot have changed speed at any time in the past. The very nature of God and His creation prohibit it.

Explanation #3 & Rebuttal

God Created Light in Transit Between the Stars and Us

According to this explanation, light was created in transit between the distant stars and us. The light we see in the night sky was created to give the appearance of these stars but did not actually ever come from them. These stars themselves do not really even need to be there at all. Indeed, according to this explanation, it is believed that exploding stars, such as the supernova observed on February 23, 1987, never existed! This particular supernova was 160,000 light-years away from us;[30] even the light from the flash which testified of the star's final death would necessarily have been created in transit. Any real light which this star's remains might have shed during the last 10,000 years would still remain in transit for the next 150,000 years.

Proponents of this "false appearance of age" theory sometimes point to the creation of Adam as an example of God's methodology.[31] They presume Adam was created with a built-in appearance of age, perhaps 20 or 30 years, but the Bible does not provide any specifics as to whether or not this is true. Because it is merely presumed to be true, it is useless as supporting evidence. Adam might have been created as a baby or even as an embryo.*

This explanation is also part of a more general theory about all scientific data indicating antiquity; according to the

---

* The embryo possibility has some fascinating scriptural support; although it would be an unnecessary and lengthy digression to examine it here, this theory may be presented in a later book.

general theory, God created the universe as it presently appears, with all of the evidence consistent with an old age built right into it.* Dinosaur bones (which are found in sediments dating much older than 10,000 years) would have been fabricated by God and planted to give the false appearance of an old earth. This would mean that they were never really part of living animals but only hints at many very interesting kinds of animals which never really existed. Also, the radioactive isotopes, which are used to date these fossils, would have been strategically planted at various levels of geological formations to give the false appearance of different ages depending on their location.

According to explanation #3, starlight speaks of an old earth but it speaks falsely. It is difficult to refute this hypothesis scientifically; all evidence would lie. Similarly, it would be difficult to prove scientifically that the universe (including our memories of it) was not just created yesterday! If we were to take this position we would have no trouble at all sidestepping any scientific evidence, but we would still have considerable difficulty with the biblical evidence.

To begin with, the thought of God fabricating and hiding dinosaur bones is strongly reminiscent of Piltdown man.[32] In 1912 a human skull was "discovered" near Piltdown, England, accompanied by a fragment of an orangutan's jaw. The jaw had been filed to imitate human tooth wear. Both the jaw and the skull had been stained to give the appearance of age. They had been buried together with some genuine ancient animal fossils—apparently as a prank. This prank got out of hand when its suspected prime perpetrator died. Any possible accomplices were, presumably, too embarrassed to confess, so the "fossil" was largely accepted by the scientific community as an ancient ancestor of man. It was not discovered to be a fraud until 1953. By then, sadly, much scientific effort had

---

* This young-earth position is different from the one which claims that the actual scientific evidence refutes the old-earth position. These two young-earth positions are in disagreement with each other over the validity of the universe's evidence.

been wasted and many men had been made to appear very foolish.

This is not the sort of thing we should suspect God of doing. It's too much like telling a lie, and God doesn't lie. The previous chapter dealt with the way in which God sometimes hides truth from people. God does not always reveal Himself in the plainest possible way, but the line must be drawn here. Explanation #3 has God fabricating false evidence. This is not the same as speaking the truth in parables or archaic language. There is no way to explain fabricated dinosaur bones or flashes from nonexistent exploding stars as hidden truth. Under explanation #3, their existence would have to be an outright deception. It simply cannot be allowed that God would bear this kind of false witness.[33] It would seem that those who have suggested this explanation have not fully thought out its consequences.

Whether the general form of this explanation is assumed, or nothing but starlight is taken to have been created with a false appearance of age, it would still be a deception. If we had never really seen the depths of the heavens but only a contrived image of them, God would not be telling us that they declare His glory (Psalm 19:1). Paul assures us that God's invisible attributes can be seen in His creation (Romans 1:20); it is certain that "liar" is *not* one of those invisible attributes; it is therefore certain that nowhere can "liar" be seen or understood from God's creation. God's very nature eliminates explanation #3 as a possibility—especially when His nature is considered in conjunction with the fact that we can read His invisible attributes in His creation.

A nonliteral meaning should never be forced on the heavens if the literal reading is consistent with the evidence. The same rules which help us interpret God's Bible must apply to His creation as well. This is especially true if the nonliteral interpretation carries the consequence that God bears a false witness in His creation.

If God's Bible had said "the universe is young" as clearly as His universe testifies it is old, then we might have to appeal to a deceptively nonliteral reading of either God's Bible or His creation. We might have to assume that God created light either between the heavens and our eyes or between our Bibles and our eyes (creating a false appearance of our Bibles). Either way, the truth is assumed to be something different from what our own eyes report to us. Fortunately, this is not our position! God has not given us any such contradiction. Both God's Bible and His creation mean *exactly* what they say; we only have to be careful and keep our eyes open when we read them.

Even if we were willing to allow this sort of deception on God's part, Einstein's theory of relativity will, once again, give us trouble. The problem is that the "false appearance of age" theory demands that the entire universe be created nearly "simultaneously."* As we have seen, the word "simultaneously" has no absolute meaning in God's universe. His time is not our time. Even in our narrow earthly frame of reference, we are still going to need billions of years of real antiquity somewhere. The problem is that "clocks" on distant quasars are marking time so slowly** that they have lagged billions of years into the past (as measured from the big bang,*** when all matter was in one place and the universe had only one frame of reference). Even under the "false appearance of age" theory, these objects exist in the very distant past when viewed from our own present frame of reference. (If you didn't follow all of this paragraph, don't worry. At least the rest of this book will be easier.)

The old-earth position is consistent with both the scientific and biblical evidence. As will be demonstrated in chapters 5 and 7, it is consistent with the scientific evidence. Chapter 7 will

---

*   In cosmological terms, six consecutive 24-hour days comprise a mere instant.

** This follows from relativity because quasars are moving away from us very rapidly.

*** The Big Bang will be explained in chapter 7.

also demonstrate that the old-earth position can be reconciled with every statement in the first chapter of Genesis.

Conclusions

All three of the suggested explanations have failed; the stars are certainly very far away from us, light has always traveled at the same speed, and God does not lie to us in His creation. There is no way light from the most distant stars could be seen from earth if the universe were very young. There are simply no other reasonable possibilities.

What this leaves is a universe which is certainly very old. There seems to be no way to compromise with the 10,000-year age proposed by the young-earth creationists. At least one of the "days" of Genesis must have been greatly longer than 24 hours. Because the young-earth creationists simply cannot be correct about this, and because the scientists have good reasons for suggesting the dates which they propose, the best course of action is to accept the scientific dates as being approximately correct.

This answers the question concerning the age of the universe as a whole but does not specifically address the question of the age of the planet Earth. Recently, some young-earth creationists have taken the position that most of the universe is very old, but the earth itself, along with its little corner of the universe, is young.[34] That argument is constructed by assuming a very unconventional configuration for the universe over time and then applying the rules governing time from relativity. Although this chapter does not address that position, the next chapter will demonstrate that the planet earth itself must be very old. Of course, if the earth is old, then that part of the universe in which it resides must also be old.

5

The Testimony of Many Witnesses

Every matter must be established by the testimony of two or three witnesses.

—2 CORINTHIANS 13:1

If the Bible does not specify that the universe is young, and if God's universe itself testifies that it is old, then the question should be settled; at least one of the "days" of Genesis 1 was a very long period of time. Still, it is likely that more proof will be needed to convince some readers. This is because many arguments have been presented in support of both positions. To many of us the universe's facts appear to be no more than a confused collection of contradictions and hence, cannot be trusted. Consider, for example, the following quotation by a young-earth creationist:

> . . . the creation model permits us to look seriously at those natural processes which seem to favor a young earth and a recent creation. We shall see later in this chapter that there exist many such processes. Unfortunately most people do not know this, since we were

all indoctrinated as children in school, with one model of origins exclusively. Only those processes which seem to favor an exceedingly old earth and old universe were included in our instruction.

—SCIENTIFIC CREATIONISM[1]

Here the claim is made that the evidence (observable processes) sometimes seems to point to a young universe and sometimes to an old one. What is really the truth? The physical universe is the work of God. Like His Bible, God's universe will always tell us the truth. Furthermore, a truthful witness can never contradict itself. This means that once the universe has clearly testified that it is either young or old, we should expect it to be completely consistent. Why, then, have we heard "scientific" arguments for both an old and a young earth?

Although the universe itself always tells the truth, those who report its facts to us will not necessarily understand them correctly. Because young-earth creationists disagree with other scientists about what the data says, it follows that one side or the other must be making mistakes. Under these circumstances we need to be careful about what we decide to believe. There will be some errors presented to us just as though they were the universe's actual facts.

The Bible provides a method for how we are to deal with a similar situation; in Deuteronomy 19:15, we are told:

> One witness is not enough to convict a man accused of any crime or offense he may have committed. A matter must be established by the testimony of two or three witnesses.

One witness would have been enough if we could be sure that he would always tell the truth, but since a witness might lie, the law tells us that we need more. If two witnesses both know and tell the truth, their testimonies will always agree with each other, but two witnesses who lie will sometimes disagree; they have no real facts with which to guide themselves.

(See Mark 14:55-59.) Of course even truthful witnesses will disagree with each other if they do not have a firm enough knowledge of the whole situation, but when this happens we cannot use their testimonies with confidence.

This chapter will examine the testimony of many "witnesses" concerning the age of God's creation. These "witnesses" will be the evidences from various scientific fields of study including tree rings, lake sediments, moon dust, volcanic action, erosion, and radioactive dating.

Tree Rings

Of the myriad ways to tell how old different things are, one of the first ones we learn, often as children, is that we can tell how old a tree is by counting its annual rings. The tree does not even need to be cut down if a thin core is taken. This method is quite easy to understand.

When a tree grows, it adds wood to its outside layer just under the bark. Trees tend to do most of their growing in the spring and summer and to sit dormantly through the winter. This means that wood is normally added to the outside of the tree in spurts once a year. These growth spurts are easily visible as annual rings in the grain of the wood. Although a tree itself may be alive, the wood at its center is actually dead. The tree is alive only on its surface where the bark is. This is why a hollow tree can survive, but removing the bark from around a tree will kill it. Each year another ring is added to the dead core of wood. Interestingly, each of the rings in a tree will actually have a slightly different carbon-14 date.

As it happens, some trees live for very long periods of time. Bristlecone pine trees, which grow in the White Mountains of California, live for many thousands of years. One lived over 5,000 years before it was, unfortunately, cut down in 1964.[2]

There is another thing, other than the age of a tree, which can be determined from studying tree rings. Scientists can determine how suitable the weather was for tree growing each year of a tree's life. During good years, most of the trees in a particular forest will add wide growth rings—during poor years, thin growth rings. Because scientists can count years (rings) backward from the present (just below the bark), they can figure, quite accurately, which years were good and which were poor for growing trees.

This effect can be used to extend the tree-ring sequence back additional thousands of years by using older dead wood which can be found on the ground. Ring patterns in the dead wood can be compared with those in living trees. Where clear evidence of overlap occurs, the ring sequence of the older dead tree can be added to the living one. Overlap can be seen since the growth patterns will be the same for any trees within a local area whose lifetimes once overlapped. This is because the weather during those years (and hence the relative widths of the related rings) would have been the same for all of those trees. By this method, the tree-ring chronology for Bristlecone pines has been extended back about 9,000 years as of 1982.[3]

Now, 9,000 years is not the age of the universe or even that of the earth. This is a minimum age for one single group of trees in California. Obviously, the soil and rocks which lie under those trees were laid down earlier still. This example was chosen as a first step because it is easy to understand (no nuclear physics involved) and because it demonstrates basic principles which will be used in some of the following examples.

Annual Layers in Sediments

Trees are not the only things in God's creation which keep a yearly record of time; sediments which accumulate in the bottoms of lakes do this, too. Different seasons create different conditions for a lake which are reflected in different types of sediment layers. In spring and summer, the layer is rich in calcium carbonate (limestone which tends to dissolve in water). Sediments from the rest of the year are rich in organic material. These layers, which are called "varves," pile up year after year and keep a record of the annual cycles. Depending on how much sedimentary matter is washed into a lake during a given year, individual annual layers can be as thin as a piece of paper or thicker than a millimeter.

The Green River Formation of Utah, Colorado, and Wyoming is estimated to contain more than four million of these annual layers.[4] They can be viewed alongside U.S. Route 191, between Duchesne and Price in Utah. The formation extends southward from the southern border of the Ashley National Forest. Because the highway drops steeply to the south, and because the layers of the formation tilt in the opposite direction, about a mile of cross-sectional thickness[5] of the formation is exposed in just a few miles of road cut. Because of variations in climate over the time the lake existed, different layers can be quite different in appearance. Some are indistinct and difficult to count, but a significant fraction of these layers (enough to prove the point all by themselves) are trivial to count (assuming a person has a great deal of time to spend); the individual layers are so sharply defined that they easily break apart into distinct flakes which are each about the thickness of a potato chip. The roadside is littered with these loose flakes which are broken off as the exposed formation weathers.

In other locations, the Green River Formation is famous for the beautiful fish, bat, crocodile, and other fossils which it contains. These fossils are all neatly arranged flatly between the layers. The sediments were obviously deposited very gently because none of the fossils cut across the layers as they would have if they had been buried suddenly. Many of the fossils also show evidence of rotting as a result of the time they spent on the bottom before being buried. Green River Formation fossils are available for inspection in museums and rock shops all over the three-state area and beyond.

Because this formation presents such an obvious proof for the antiquity of the earth, young-earth creationists have attempted to suggest ways these layers might have formed quickly; however, none of the suggestions are plausible. For example, these layers did not result from an erupting volcano like Mt. St. Helens. Although volcanos can generate striped patterns in the ash they expel, it hardly needs mentioning that this ash is never comprised of calcium carbonate or neatly interlayered with fish fossils. Furthermore, the Green River Formation contains two thin layers which really are volcanic in origin.[6] These two layers are distinguishable from the rest of the formation only because the rest of the formation is comprised of lake-bottom sediments rather than more of the same volcanic material.

The Green River Formation is obviously not a volcanic artifact, but is it possible that these layers were all deposited during the single year of Noah's flood? In order to deposit four million layers in one year, the layers must be deposited faster than one every eight seconds! The problem becomes one of changing the composition of the fine-grained sedimentary particles in an area about the size of Lake Erie from limestone to organic then back to limestone again, once every eight seconds. Furthermore, this must be done without disturbing the water so much that fine-grained sediments cannot settle out of it. This is clearly not what the evidence is telling us either.

If we assume that the layers were deposited naturally over 10,000 years (ignoring Noah's flood and the fact that the lake vanished long ago), and if we assume the layers somehow formed slightly faster than one per day, then we would still need to account for the mile depth of the formation. The Mississippi and Colorado rivers, taken together, drain about half of the area of the continental United States (excluding Alaska), and both are well known for the large amount of silt they carry. Together, they transport less than a tenth of a cubic mile of sediment per year.[7] If we made the impossible assumption that both of those rivers dumped their entire sediment load into this one lake and that no sediments ever washed out of it, this would only add about half an inch per year spread over the roughly 10,000-square-mile lake bottom. Even with these unreasonably extreme assumptions we cannot explain the evidence we see; in 10,000 years, this would account for less than a tenth of the formation's thickness.

On the other hand, annual seasonal cycles are a natural, observable, built-in feature of God's creation, and perfectly reasonable assumptions about sedimentation rates will account for every bit of physical evidence, *if* we do not insist the earth is young. The only reasonable reading of the evidence is that the layers resulted from a lake which existed for millions of years. There is no easy way to misunderstand this evidence. And this is still not the age of the earth; it is only the length of time one particular lake existed. This evidence, and the evidence of starlight from the previous chapter, establishes that the earth and universe must be millions of years old at the very least.*

Moon Dust

Young-earth creationists argue that scientists only concentrate on those methods of dating which yield old ages, arbitrarily ignoring any method which does not give an old enough age. One young-earth argument involves moon dust. Because this argument has often been cited, it will be examined in some detail.

The amount of dust on the surface of the moon has been presented as evidence that the universe is young. This argument begins with the estimate that a large quantity of meteoric dust falls onto the earth each year. Assuming that the rate of dust falling onto the moon is about the same as that estimated for the earth, it would seem that there should be a great deal of dust piled up on the moon. Based on this, it is argued that there is insufficient dust on the moon's surface if the moon is billions of years old.

---

* Other evidence, such as light from astronomical objects more distant than M31, establishes that the universe is actually billions of years old.

Unlike the moon, the earth is an active environment. Therefore, the dust which settles onto it does not form an undisturbed layer. What has happened to this dust on the earth will be briefly considered at the end of this chapter. Arguments from two different young-earth sources concerning the moon's dust will be examined here:

Source #1

> Hans Pettersson of the Swedish Oceanographic Institute calculated that about 14.3 million tons of meteoritic dust of the type which contain nickel settles to earth each year. Isaac Asimov has calculated that, if this rate has continued unaltered for the past 5 billion years, then there should be a layer of meteoric dust at least 54 feet thick all over the earth. No such layer is found.[8]

> Prior to our first manned moon landing, some NASA scientists predicted that there might be as much as 54 feet of this lunar soil, assuming the age of the moon to be about 5 billion years and assuming that meteorites had been falling on the moon at the present rate since or near the beginning of its birth.[9] We now know that no such thick surface layer exists. Instead, the most recent estimates of average regolith thickness are as follows:

> (a) Near the Apollo 11 site, in the Sea of Tranquility, 13 feet.

> (b) Near the Apollo 12 site, in the Ocean of Storms, 11 1/2 feet.

> (c) Near the Luna 16 site, in the Sea of Fertility, 2-3 feet. (According to theory, Fertility soil should have been thicker than the other since it is an "older" area.)

> It appears that this "timer," the build-up of moon soil, has not been "running" for about 5 billion years, but rather, has only recently been "turned on."[10]
>
> —SCIENCE AND CREATION

Source #2

It is known that there is essentially a constant rate of cosmic dust particles entering the earth's atmosphere from space and then gradually settling to the earth's surface. The best measurements of this influx have been made by Hans Pettersson, who obtained the figure of 14 million tons per year. This amounts to 14×10^{19} pounds in 5 billion years. If we assume the density of compacted dust is, say, 140 pounds per cubic foot, this corresponds to a volume of 10^{18} cubic feet. Since the earth has a surface area of approximately 5.5×10^{15} square feet, this seems to mean that there should have accumulated during the 5-billion-year age of the earth, a layer of meteoric dust approximately 182 feet thick all over the world!

There is not the slightest sign of such a dust layer anywhere of course. On the moon's surface it should be at least as thick, but the astronauts found no sign of it (before the moon landings, there was considerable fear that the men would sink into the dust when they arrived on the moon, but no comment has apparently ever been made by the authorities as to why it wasn't there as anticipated).

—SCIENTIFIC CREATIONISM[11]

In summary, the claims about moon dust (which is also called lunar soil or regolith) are as follows:

Moon Dust Claims:

1) Based on Hans Pettersson's earth-based measurements of meteoric influx there should be at least 54 feet of dust on the surface of the earth—or at least 182 feet depending upon whose estimate we use. A layer at least as thick should be on the surface of the moon.

2) The depth of this dust is 13 feet near the Apollo 11 site, in the Sea of Tranquility; 11 1/2 feet near the Apollo 12 site, in the Ocean of Storms; and 2 to 3 feet near the Luna 16 site, in the Sea of Fertility.

3) According to theory, the soil at the Sea of Fertility should have been thicker than the other areas since it is an "older" area.

4) The astronauts found no sign of this heavy dust layer and authorities have not commented as to why it wasn't there as anticipated.

Difficulties emerge as we compare these various claims with other information, including NASA's testimony about the Apollo flights.

Claim #1: Earth-based measurements predict a great deal of dust on the moon.

This claim says that dust is falling onto the earth at a rate which would have resulted in a very deep pile if it were left undisturbed over billions of years (no rain washing it away, no volcanos burying it, and so on). Because the surface of the moon has been left virtually undisturbed—there is no weather there—this dust should be visible there if the universe is very old.

The problem is the data used to calculate the 54-foot or 182-foot depths is out of date. Recent measurements tell us that this influx to the earth is actually 1,000 times less than Pettersson originally estimated back in 1960.[12] Clearly this first claim is an error. It is based on very obsolete data. It follows that the moon must also receive less dust.

Many different determinations of the influx to the moon's surface have been made which confirm this. These include influx samples taken at the moon by the Apollo astronauts using collector targets and also pieces of the Surveyor III spacecraft which were recovered by a later flight and examined for micrometeorites.[13] The evidence confirms that very little meteoric dust actually falls onto the moon.

The next two claims will be taken in reverse order to simplify things.

Claim #3: According to theory, the soil at the Sea of Fertility should have been thicker than soil at the other areas since it is an "older" area.

This claim gets progressively weaker the closer it is traced to its source. The publication which the authors of *Science and Creation* are quoting is the January 23, 1971 issue of *Science News* where three soil depths (of Claim #2) are given in a brief news item with a comment on the fact that the Luna 16 core presented some surprises. From this 35-centimeter (14-inch) core the Soviet scientist Vinogradov concluded that the depth of the dust was "possibly 0.5 to 1 meter."[14] Notice his use here of the word "possibly." This puts the evidence in a less-definite light.

Three pages earlier in the same issue of *Science News,* we see how Vinogradov arrived at this conclusion. "The Luna 16 drill hit a solid object (which he says could have been bedrock)."[15] It is also possible that the solid object was nothing more than a large buried rock. Luna 16 was unmanned and so it only had one chance to take its sample; it had no way to walk over a few feet and try again.

Although it is claimed that Fertility soil should have been thicker than soil from the other areas, since it is an "older" area, it is not clear that Fertility soil isn't deeper. As this fact has been traced back toward its source, it looks less like proof that the scientists were wrong about moon dust, and more like one Soviet probe may have had the bad luck of hitting a rock after drilling only about 14 inches.

Claim #2: The dust on the moon at three locations was 13, 11.5, and 2-3 feet deep.

The Luna 16 data point (the two-to-three-foot-deep one) has already been examined. *Science News* did not specify whether the Apollo 11 and 12 cores (the other two locations mentioned here) actually bottomed out against bedrock or whether the numbers given were just the length of the cores taken and, hence, would only indicate a minimum depth. In any case, more recent Apollo flights tell us much more.

By the time of the Apollo 16 flight, some more sophisticated experiments had been performed. In NASA's preliminary report on the Apollo 16 mission, results of a seismic experiment are given which place the depth of the lunar soil at about 12.2 meters (40 feet).[16]

This large depth could not easily have been determined by merely driving a core rod through it. The astronauts had great difficulty driving even a 10-foot core into the moon's soil;[17] in the moon's low gravity it was hard for the astronauts to press downward, and the moon dust presented an unexpected amount of resistance. The lunar soil is not exposed to weathering effects so the individual grains are jagged and catch on each other. Footprints sink into it less than they would into sand on a beach. This is why the astronaut's footprints were so shallow.

Finally, consider the NASA report titled *The Soviet-American Conference On Cosmochemistry of the Moon and Planets.*[18] This report is a source which, in my opinion, contains everything anyone would want to know about meteoric influx and the depth of moon dust. As this report explains on page 574, the moon's "maria" (the darker, more recently melted areas) have dust piled several meters thick over them, but its "continental regions" are piled as deeply as dozens of meters thick[19]—this would be about 100 feet.[20]

Also in this same NASA report, the effect of the falling meteoric dust on the soil is shown in terms of the amount of mixing of the soil over various time spans. The falling dust, at present-day rates, is so low that it would have taken a billion years to have even stirred up the moon's top 10 centimeters (4 inches).[21] As it turns out, this rate has not been constant over the moon's lifetime; it will be seen in chapter 7 that, because of the way God created our solar system, the amount of falling dust would have been much greater in the early days while the solar system (the earth, sun, moon, and planets) was still being formed.

Claim #4: Astronauts found no sign of this dust and no comment has been made by the authorities as to why it wasn't there as anticipated.

This claim is clearly in error. A great deal of dust covers the moon; NASA has released reams of information concerning it. This information is sufficient in scope and detail to bore a researcher to tears. Of course not *all* of this information was available back in 1973 and 1974 when these moon-dust arguments were originally composed, but it is certainly available to us now.*

In conclusion, it is obvious that the amount of dust on the moon does not indicate a young earth. The testimonies of some young-earth creationists have been compared with the testimony of NASA and were found to disagree. Because everyone must get their information indirectly through NASA, the error must be in the young-earth testimonies. There is nowhere else, other than the moon landings, that they could obtain their information.

Volcanos and Erosion

There are right and wrong ways to read the Bible. One wrong way is to take a single verse out of context and ignore the rest of Scripture. The only correct way to study the Bible is to examine *all* of the scriptural evidence. The same rule also applies to the study of God's creation. The following will compare the testimonies of two young-earth arguments to illustrate a failure to study God's creation in its full context. The first argument concerns how much mass is being added to the continents each year by volcanic activity:

> . . . it seems reasonable to assume that at least 10 cubic kilometers of new igneous rocks are formed each year by flows from the earth's mantle.

---

* The Apollo 16 information was available back in 1972.

> The total volume of the earth's crust is about 5×10^9 cubic kilometers. Thus, the entire crust could have been formed by volcanic activity at present rates in only 500 million years, which would only take us back into the Cambrian period. On the other hand, all geologists would surely agree that practically all the earth's crust had been formed billions of years before that time. The uniformitarian model once again leads to a serious problem and contradiction.
>
> —SCIENTIFIC CREATIONISM[22]

Because volcanic rock is being continuously added to the earth's crust, and because only so much crust has piled up, we are expected to conclude that the earth must be young. This argument is quite easy to understand and sounds valid, but it represents a single scientific fact being removed from the context of other related scientific facts. What is worse, the critical scientific context from which this has been removed was presented only two pages earlier in the same book:

> Approximately 27.5 billion tons of sediment are being transported to the ocean every year. The total mass of sediments already in the ocean is about 820 million billion tons. Dividing the total mass by the transport rate yields 30 million years as the maximum age of the ocean since sediments first started to flow into it . . . the total mass of continental rocks above sea level is only about 383 million billion tons . . . Thus, in only 383/27.5, or 14, million years, the present continents, eroding at present rates, would have been eroded to sea level![23]

Here also we are told that there is an upper limit to how old the earth can be. Otherwise, all of the dirt that exists would have washed down into the ocean by now. This argument would also look good if it were taken all by itself, but notice what happens to the two arguments when they are examined together in the greater context which their combined information provides.

In the first argument, we are told that each year volcanic activity adds at least 10 cubic kilometers to the earth's crust; in the second, we are told that each year rivers are washing 27.5 billion tons of this away. These two work out to be the same amount—the two processes balance each other almost exactly.[24]

This material finally settles to the ocean floor, but it does not remain there forever. The sea floor is not stationary; it slides around, riding on the slowly moving plates of rock which make up the earth's surface. Sediments are ultimately carried back down into the hot interior parts of the earth.[25] Some of this material eventually gets recycled by volcanic activity; it completes the cycle by returning to the earth's crust, only to be washed away again.

So what has happened to the two arguments? Both have been shown to be worthless. Their supporting scientific evidence has simply been taken out of the context of the full testimony of the earth's evidence.

One might just as well have argued that the earth must be young because "All streams flow into the sea, yet the sea is never full" (Ecclesiastes 1:7), but as Solomon continues and explains: "To the place the streams come from, there they return again" (also Ecclesiastes 1:7). God designed the world in such a way that it can operate well for a long time. As Paul said, the creation was made to reflect the invisible attributes of its Creator (Romans 1:20) and He is not about to run down either.

Again, when witnesses for the young-earth position are examined, errors are found in their testimony. I do not believe that men who have presented these arguments are deliberately trying to deceive people; however, it is inescapable that they have not been as careful in checking things out as they should have been.

Radioactive Dating

Another witness to the great age of the earth is the evidence from radioactive isotopes—radiation dating. It almost seems like no creationist's book is complete without a chapter devoted to pointing out its problems—often imaginary ones. In this book, radiation dating will be explained in enough detail that you can get a feel of where problems exist and where they do not. Where the problems are not significant, radioactive dating becomes another of the universe's witnesses to the truth. Anything that can be used to help determine the truth is really on our side!

Different types of radioactive dating are useful for different situations and age ranges. Some types of uranium, for example, can be used to date very old things* (ages in billions of years, such as the solar system). However, these are not very useful for more recent things (mere millions of years). The potassium-argon method is good for the millions-to-billions-of-years range; recent improvements have made it accurate to about the nearest 10,000 years. Unfortunately, it can only be used on volcanic materials; one is not likely to find a handy lava flow in the vicinity of, and within 100,000 years of, a fossil which one might be trying to date. For this reason, it is generally not useful for dating specimens younger than about half a million years of age. Carbon-14 has a useful range which includes most fossils identified as modern men. This makes it useful to archaeologists.

Carbon-14

Normal, everyday carbon-12 has six protons and six neutrons.** Six plus six is twelve, which is why it is called carbon-12. (The electrons are not counted here.) Carbon-14 has six protons (like carbon-12) but eight neutrons—which totals fourteen. Carbon-12 is stable, which means that it lasts forever.

---

* Because the uranium dating method is very involved, we will not go into it here. Determining the original quantities involves correlating many different isotope concentrations.

** Carbon (including both normal C-12 and radioactive C-14) is the stuff that coal, graphite (pencil "lead"), and diamonds are made of. It is also a major part of gasoline, limestone, sugar, fireplace ashes, and every living creature.

Carbon-14 is not, which means that it changes into something else when given enough time. One of the extra neutrons in carbon-14 will suddenly split apart into an electron (which we will ignore) and a proton (which we won't). This means there will then be seven protons and seven neutrons. An atom having seven protons and seven neutrons is not carbon, but nitrogen (specifically nitrogen-14).

The rate at which carbon-14 turns into nitrogen-14 has been accurately measured in laboratories and has been found to be quite constant. Decay rates are constant under all conditions for which life is possible; altering those rates takes heroic effort. They can be altered by only a small fraction of a percent with pressures so great that the very atoms themselves begin to crush (over one million pounds per square inch).[26] Although rates can be changed significantly by intense neutron radiation,[27] this generates different decay products than normally would be formed; this means there would be evidence if this happened.[28]

What has been found, based on laboratory measurements, is that after a period of about 5,770 years, half of the atoms in a lump of pure carbon-14 will turn into nitrogen-14. This is called its "half-life." In another 5,770 years, half of the remaining half will also turn into nitrogen-14 (*not all* of the remaining half) and so on. After three half-lives, only 1/8 of the original carbon-14 would remain. The nitrogen produced eventually escapes into the air, which is mostly nitrogen anyway.

Now, if we could know how much carbon-14 was in a particular sample at the beginning (for C-14 this corresponds to the time when a particular living thing died), the remaining amount could be used to figure out how long that sample had been around. If only one fourth of the original C-14 remained, then it would follow that the original amount had been reduced by half, two times. This would mean that the sample had been sitting for 5,770 + 5,770 years, or 11,540 years.

As with any useful radioactive-dating method, it turns out there *is* a way to figure out how much of the important components were originally present. Otherwise the method would be unusable. As we will see, the amount of carbon-14 originally present in a plant or animal at the moment of its death can be determined from the amount of carbon-12 which is still present in that specimen.

New carbon-14 is constantly being produced from nitrogen-14 by cosmic rays in the upper atmosphere at about the same rate at which the old carbon-14 is decaying back into nitrogen. The rate of production does change a little from year to year and from century to century, but the ratio between the number of C-12 atoms and C-14 atoms in the air is, more or less, always constant. What variation there is will be considered later.

The newly formed carbon-14 quickly reacts with oxygen to form carbon dioxide. This carbon dioxide is continually taken from the air by plants and converted into other things such as sugar and oxygen. This is how plants grow. They build themselves up from atoms, including the carbon which they get from the carbon dioxide in the air, and from other atoms which they get from soil and water. Similarly, animals eat the plants and therefore build themselves from the same atoms. Even carnivores, which eat other animals instead of plants, ultimately get their carbon from the air through the herbivores they eat. This means that whatever C-12/C-14 ratio happens to be in the air at any given time is the same as the C-12/C-14 ratio which exists in all living plants and animals at that time.

When a plant or animal dies, it stops eating and breathing, so it no longer exchanges its carbon with the carbon in the air. This means that the C-14 slowly starts to disappear (by turning into nitrogen gas) while the C-12 stays put. Furthermore, because C-12 and C-14 are chemically identical, any chemical reaction which might remove the C-14 from a specimen will also remove the C-12 by the same fractional amount. This will have no effect on the calculated date.

In a laboratory, the amounts of C-12 and C-14 can be accurately measured. Because C-12 lasts forever, the amount of it in a fossil animal is the same as the amount it had when it died. Because we know approximately how many C-14 atoms were originally present for every C-12 atom, it follows that we can calculate the original amount of C-14. Thus we have everything we need to figure out how long ago the specimen died.

There are still some problems. One is that the sample can be contaminated by other material containing carbon with a different C-12/C-14 ratio. When we closely examine an old bone, we notice that it is full of little holes like a sponge. This means that it can soak things up. Teeth, tusks, and antlers are also porous. This does not make the C-14 method unusable. It just means that scientists have to be a little more careful when they try to date this type of specimen. Limestone, which also contains carbon, will often soak into these holes during the thousands of years while a sample is buried. When this happens, it must be washed out before accurate dating can be done. Acid is used for this wash because limestone dissolves readily in acid while bones, teeth, tusks, and antlers do not.

This acid wash was apparently misunderstood in one young-earth argument which claimed that "Yale University dated an antler three different times and got three different ages—5,340 years, 9,310 years, and 10,320 years."[29] We might picture in our minds a very confused scientist until we check the original source where we find that the three dates were these: the antler when it was contaminated with recently formed limestone—9,310 years; the antler after the limestone had been washed out—10,320 years; and the limestone itself which had been washed out into the acid—5,340 years.[30] When we look more closely, this turns out to be a perfectly reasonable set of measurements.[31]

Another type of contamination occurs when an animal eats very old, rotten vegetation instead of fresh. If a living mollusk—a type of animal including aquatic (water-living) snails—eats only muck which has been dead for thousands of years, it will eventually carbon-14 date the same age as that muck. This is common for bottom-feeding snails which live in muddy rivers where very old sediments are constantly being churned up. According to C-14's theoretical basis, "You are what you eat"; for these snails, this can be vegetation which has been dead for 3,000 years. This is not usually a problem because most animals are more careful about what they eat. Neither is this a problem for aquatic snails which live in clear lakes or in the ocean.[32]

One other problem is that scientists don't know exactly how many C-14 per C-12 atoms there were in the atmosphere during every century all the way back through time, but they are starting to work their way back. They are finding this out by carbon-14 dating wood from very old trees. The real age of this wood is determined by counting tree rings.* In this manner, carbon-14 dating has been checked back more than 7,000 years as of 1971.[33] As of 1982, the ring sequence was extended back to about 9,000 years ago.

As a result of testing tree rings, it was found that carbon-14 dates had been slightly in error (about 15 percent off for a 7,000-year-old specimen) due to the differing rates of atmospheric C-14 production in past ages. However, the observed error was not in the direction which would suggest a young earth. What had previously been measured and thought to be a mere 6,000 years old was now known to be about 7,000 years old. Now that the direction and amount of this error is known, the information is used to correct modern C-14 dates and thereby make them more accurate.

---

* A tree will almost always add a single growth ring every year, and, of course, scientists have been careful to make due provision for both missing and duplicate annual growth rings.

Other checks have been made still farther back. For example, a C-14 date of 45,000 years was cross-checked with one of the uranium-dating systems with less than a 4 percent difference.[34] Here we cannot know which of the two dates (or both) is in error.* Although by no means conclusive, this check is at least a good sign.

In specimens from as far back in time as 50,000 years, less than one-fourth of 1 percent of the original C-14 still remains. This makes accurate measurement quite difficult. With the present state of the art, carbon-14 dates of greater than 50,000 years are not accurate enough to be useful. It is not expected that the C-14 method will ever be refined to a level where it can be used to date material older than 100,000 years.[35]

A specimen becomes too old to be dated by the C-14 method when most of its C-14 has decayed away. Coal, for example, has virtually no C-14 remaining. This means that it is impossible to assign a date to coal using this method—except to say that it must be older than C-14's useful range. It is just not possible to calculate how much older.

In summary, with a reasonable amount of caution, and with moderate corrections for known past variations, carbon-14 can be a useful method for dating organic specimens as old as 9,000 years with a high level of confidence. The method can be tested this far back. At present, the method can be extended to an upper limit of about 50,000 years with increasingly reduced confidence.

The Dating Gap

There is a period called "the dating gap" which is considered very difficult to date. It extends from where C-14 drops off to where the potassium-argon method becomes useful—dates in the hundreds of thousands of years. Techniques for dating this period are still under development.[36] For the

---

* With C-14 and tree rings, it was understood that the error was in the C-14 date and not in the tree ring count.

present, we will do well to be suspicious of dates which fall into this time period.

Potassium-Argon

For older dates (hundreds of thousands of years or more) potassium-argon starts to become an effective way to date volcanic materials. The way this method works is that radioactive potassium-40 (potassium is a common mineral element) decays into argon-40 (argon is an inert gas). The argon will become trapped[37] inside the rock crystals where the potassium was. The decay mechanism is similar to carbon-14's but it happens at a much slower rate;[38] it takes 1.3 billion years for half of the potassium-40 to change into argon. This is one reason why potassium-argon (K-Ar) is only useful for such old dates.

Another property of K-Ar dating is that a volcano must erupt to reset its clock to zero. Because this does not happen very often in most parts of the world, it is not always possible to use K-Ar dating to assign precise dates. Individual eruptions in one location might be hundreds of thousands or many millions of years apart.

When a volcanic sample is heated to melting (this is the condition of hot lava from an erupting volcano), all of the argon-40 is driven out of it.[39] Because argon is inert, it cannot react with or combine with hot volcanic rock at all. Instead, the argon is boiled completely out of the rock and released into the atmosphere. This means that every time a volcano erupts and ejects hot lava or ash, the lava and ash will have no argon in them. This is how a volcano resets the K-Ar clock; no argon means that no time has elapsed since the eruption which ejected the particular sample.

This is certainly true at the earth's surface, but if a volcano erupts far beneath the surface of the ocean, the tremendous pressure at this depth can prevent the argon from completely escaping. The resulting error can be more than 20 million years of false age when the water is a few miles deep.[40] Because of this, we should allow for the possibility that underwater K-Ar dates might appear significantly older than they really are. However, this is not a problem with surface volcanos, nor does this amount of error appear to be very significant when one is dealing with ages ranging in the hundreds of millions of years.

A similar problem occurs when volcanic materials become buried very deeply beneath the earth's surface. If it is hot enough where they are buried, volcanic materials can become partially remelted, allowing some argon to escape. This can reset the K-Ar clock, although not necessarily all the way back to zero. For this reason, K-Ar measurements on metamorphic rocks (rocks which have been reshaped by heat and pressure) are not considered by scientists to be reliable. Of course this effect makes rocks appear younger than they really are instead of older.

From the time of a volcanic eruption onward, any argon in an uncontaminated ash sample has to have been produced by decaying potassium—at least for surface volcanos. By measuring the amount of potassium-40 in the sample and the amount of argon which is released when the sample is reheated in a laboratory, we can determine when a particular eruption occurred. The more argon present, the longer ago it happened.

Until very recently, K-Ar dates have typically been accurate only to within about plus or minus 100,000 years. Because of the small amounts of argon involved, even very small amounts of contamination caused problems.* Even the best dates were no better than plus or minus 50,000 years[41] and much greater errors often resulted when scientists became careless. Recent improvements in technology, involving lasers to test a single crystal of rock at a time, have enabled scientists to make measurements with accuracies as good as plus or minus 10,000

---

* A small amount of contamination is almost inevitable because there is some argon present in the atmosphere.

years on volcanic materials which are three million years old.[42] This is better than 1 percent accuracy.

Also, a new dating technique which claims astronomical synchronization is beginning to make it possible to cross-check K-Ar dates. The method is still in its infancy and so it is being regarded with some caution. Its initial results agree to within about 7 percent of the K-Ar dates.[43]

The K-Ar method is useful for determining the ages of the various strata in a segment of the geologic column. When a volcano erupts, ash is spread over a large area of ground. Later, it may become buried. If volcanic ash can be found between layers of earth, then a real date can usually be assigned to that level of the column. A scientist will know that any fossil found "below"* that level is older than the ash. That fossil must have been buried before the volcano erupted or the ash would not have fallen on layers above it. Likewise the scientist knows that fossils which he finds in layers "above" the ash are more recent. Occasionally a scientist will be lucky enough to find a fossil sandwiched closely between two datable layers and can know the age of his find quite accurately.[44]

Potassium-argon dating can also be useful in determining how various parts of the earth have moved around during past ages. The continental masses are gradually drifting around, sometimes colliding with each other, sometimes splitting apart. As a result, over the years the "geologic column" has been broken into many large and small pieces. Also, wind and water erode away some top layers, leaving others, and deposit the rubble elsewhere. Dating a vertical sequence of lava flows can help a geologist to determine how the various pieces fit together. Of course there is a good deal of other evidence to help him—such as the visible presence of fault lines.

Working out the particular geology of an area is always a necessary first step before any fossils can be reliably dated

---

* The terms "above" and "below" refer to the time when the earth's layers were originally laid down. In some cases, such as when faulting occurs, the earth can shift around and make these directions difficult to discern.

using the potassium-argon method.[45] This can be either an easy or difficult task depending on how broken up the terrain is or how visible the various layers are. At many places such as the Grand Canyon, where all of the layers are orderly and exposed for observation, this task can be trivial. At other places, where faulting has displaced the layers and they are only sporadically visible, the task can be quite difficult. Of course, the volcanic materials themselves can always be dated without knowledge of the surrounding geology.

Young-earth creationists often claim that the geological time scale was worked out by evolutionists before radioactive dating was even invented—that the presently assigned dates, therefore, really have nothing to do with radioactive-dating methods at all.[46] This claim ignores the fact that when radioactive dating did become available, scientists discovered that the first guesses (based on faulty assumptions) had been greatly in error and so the dates were corrected. For example, the Miocene, formerly thought to have begun less than a million years ago, was found to have begun more than 20 million years earlier![47] Here the true date was 20 times more ancient than the original estimate! The presently accepted dates have very little in common with the earlier ones.

In summary, potassium-argon is a useful method for dating volcanic materials which are older than a few hundred thousand years, which were erupted from surface volcanos, and which have not been buried too deeply. Measurements made many years ago will not be more accurate than plus or minus 50,000 years; in extreme cases, they can be much worse. More recent measurements can be as accurate as plus or minus 10,000 years. If fossils are to be dated by this method, the surrounding geology must be understood. Volcanic materials which were erupted into deep oceans might date much older than they really are; deeply buried rocks might date much younger.

Fission-Track Dating

Even with its problems, K-Ar dating is a useful tool for determining the ages of various events in the earth's history. However, for those readers who are still concerned about the problems of contamination or escaping daughter products, the fission-track method may provide a better answer.[48]

Fission-track dating can be used on tiny Zircon crystals which are found in volcanic ash. These crystals contain a small amount of uranium-238, which decays into lead. Unlike most other radioactive elements, U-238 releases a significant amount of energy when it decays—enough that the emitted particles actually plow through the surrounding crystal. These plow marks, called fission tracks, are visible in a carefully polished and etched crystal; they can be individually counted under a microscope.

The fission-track clock is started when a new Zircon crystal forms. A newly formed crystal will have no plow marks. As time passes, some of the available atoms of uranium decay—each plowing a new fission track. The amount of U-238 in the crystal determines the rate at which new tracks appear. The more time that has passed since a crystal was formed, the more fission tracks will be present in that crystal.

Because fission tracks are merely scratches which are buried inside an otherwise unmarred crystal, there is no way they can leak into or out of it. (Once a scratch has been made, it stays put.) This makes the dating method immune to contamination or leakage. Since the amount of U-238 in the crystal can be determined by laboratory analysis and because the decay rate of U-238 is known,[49] the amount of time since a Zircon crystal was formed can always be determined. Nothing else has a significant effect on the determined date.

More Examples

I have spent a great deal of time investigating young-earth arguments, but I have never found a single argument which stood up when studied in context with a more complete understanding of the scientific evidence which God's creation provides. To drive the point home, here are some more examples:

(1) There is insufficient meteoric dust mixed into the earth's crust if it is old. (See *Scientific Creationism*, ed. Henry M. Morris, Ph.D., © 1974, Master Books, El Cajon, CA, pp. 151-153.)

As we have seen earlier in this chapter, there is 1,000 times less meteoric influx to the earth than was assumed for that calculation. There are also processes at work removing this dust. Soil is constantly being washed into the oceans, deposited on the sea floors, and then the sea floors themselves are continuously being pulled down into the earth's mantle. Meteoric elements easily combine with iron and so they are ultimately scavenged into the earth's core. (See *The Cambridge Encyclopedia of Earth Sciences*, ed. David G. Smith, Ph.D., © 1981, Crown Publishers Inc./Cambridge University Press, New York, pp. 33,58.)

(2) It used to be argued that the sun is shrinking too rapidly—that it would have been larger in the past than the earth's orbit if the earth is old—but this argument is presently losing support. (See *It's a Young World After All, Exciting Evidences for Recent Creation*, Paul D. Ackerman, © 1986, Baker Book House, Grand Rapids, MI 49506, pp. 61-63.)

The measuring technique was changed (giving the sun a different *apparent* size), but the sun's actual size seems to have stayed the same. If the sun had really been as much larger in the past as this argument claimed, *some historically recorded total eclipses would have been impossible.* (See "The Consistency of the Solar Diameter Over the Past 250 Years," John H. Parkinson, Leslie V. Morrison and F. Richard Stephenson, *Nature*, December 11, 1980, vol. 288, pp. 548,549.)

(3) Comets are short-lived; when they are near the sun, various forces break them apart, leaving a trail of debris behind. There are too many comets still orbiting the sun if the solar system is old. (See *Scientific Creationism*, ed. Henry M. Morris, Ph.D., © 1974, Master Books, El Cajon, CA, p. 158.)

New comets are continuously being introduced into our solar system from beyond Pluto's orbit. When far away from the sun, comets are not short lived. (See *Mysteries of the Universe*, Nigel Henbest, © 1981, Van Nostrand Reinhold Company, New York, p. 22.) Recent astronomical observations with the Hubble Space Telescope (and earlier observations with a 2.2-meter telescope on Mauna Kea in Hawaii) have even located one of the sources of new comets. (See "Beyond Neptune," John Horgan, *Scientific American*, October 1995, vol. 273, no. 4, pp. 24,26.)

(4) The solar wind blows small particles of cosmic dust out of the solar system while the Poynting-Robertson effect causes larger particles to be dragged into the sun. There should no longer be any debris left in the solar system if it is old. (See *The Creation-Evolution Controversy*, Randy L. Wysong, © 1976, Inquiry Press, 4925 Jefferson Ave., Midland, MI 48640, pp. 169-171. See also *Handy Dandy Evolution Refuter*, Robert E. Kofahl, © 1977, Beta Books, San Diego, CA, p. 127.)

Comets are constantly littering up the inner solar system with debris stripped off them by the solar wind and other forces. This replaces the debris which is removed. (See *The Creation-Evolution Controversy*, Randy L. Wysong, © 1976, Inquiry Press, 4925 Jefferson Ave., Midland, MI 48640, p. 168. See also *Handy Dandy Evolution Refuter*, Robert E. Kofahl, © 1977, Beta Books, San Diego, CA, p. 126.) The debris left behind the 1910 pass of Halley's Comet still causes meteor showers every time the earth passes through the comet's path.

(5) Underground gas and oil are often under great pressure, but studies of the permeability of the surrounding rocks show that the pressure *should have bled off too quickly* for the earth to be old. (See *The Creation-Evolution Controversy*, Randy L. Wysong, © 1976, Inquiry Press, 4925 Jefferson Ave., Midland, MI 48640, p. 159.)

Pressure does not leak *out* of underground gas and oil reservoirs, it leaks *into* them. Because rocks are permeable, because ground water fills the pores in them, and because the reservoirs are deep in the earth, an oil or gas reservoir will normally be under about as much pressure as if it were under an equivalent depth of sea water. If the pressure is released from a reservoir through a well and then the well is resealed, seeping water will bring the pressure back up to this level within a few days or weeks depending on the permeability of the surrounding rocks. (See *Petroleum Engineering*, Alfred Mayer-Gurr, © 1976, Ferdinand Enke Publishers, Stuttgart, pp. 59,127,128.)

(6) Even if a planet or moon is created so hot that it is molten, it will cool with time, yet many astronomical bodies are still very hot in their interiors. Jupiter's moon Io and the earth are two examples whose interiors are still hot enough to support active volcanos. This would not be possible if the solar system were as old as scientists claim. (For the "Io" argument, see *It's a Young World After All, Exciting Evidences for Recent Creation*, Paul D. Ackerman, © 1986, Baker Book House, Grand Rapids, MI 49506, pp. 43-44. For the "earth" argument, see *The Creation-Evolution Controversy*, Randy L. Wysong, © 1976, Inquiry Press, 4925 Jefferson Ave., Midland, MI 48640, p. 171-172.)

In the case of the earth, the radioactive uranium, thorium, and potassium in its interior are estimated to produce about 9.5×10^{20} joules/year of heat energy. This is sufficient to keep it hot inside. (See *The Cambridge Encyclopedia of Earth Sciences,* ed. David G. Smith, Ph.D., © 1981, Crown Publishers Inc./Cambridge University Press, New York, p. 151.) Furthermore, the composition of the interior of any moon or planet other than the earth is almost completely unknown; they might contain radioactive elements just like the earth does. Jupiter's moon Io is very close to Jupiter and therefore experiences strong tidal flexing from Jupiter's strong gravity. Like anything that is flexed enough, this will make it hot. (See "Jupiter, Not Bust," Fred Guterl, *Discover,* January 1997, vol. 18, no. 1, p. 43.) Interestingly, the volcanos on Io were *predicted* by calculations of these tidal forces before they were discovered. (See *Cosmos,* Carl Sagan, © 1980, Random House, New York, p. 157.)

(7) Material taken from the surface of the earth's moon was found to be very high in radioactivity. It is argued from this that the moon could not even be millions of years old or it would have melted by this time; some even argue that the moon has a cool interior. (See *The Creation-Evolution Controversy,* Randy L. Wysong, © 1976, Inquiry Press, 4925 Jefferson Ave., Midland, MI 48640, p. 177.) But the opposite argument is made by other young-earth creationists: The moon has a hot interior; since it has not cooled off yet, it cannot be billions of years old. (See *In the Beginning,* Walter T. Brown Jr., Center for Scientific Creation, 5612 20th Place, Phoenix, AZ 85016, pp. 18,54.)

Both arguments cannot possibly be correct. Whatever temperature the moon's interior is, it cannot be both cool and hot. Again, it appears the young-earth creationists have been careless in gathering their facts and also have failed to take all of the information into account. The moon is heated by radioactive materials (although the composition of the moon below its surface is still poorly known), but it also loses heat into space (by infrared radiation) as any warm object does.

(8) Meteorites have supposedly been falling during the entire history of the earth. There would be large numbers of them preserved in the geologic column if the earth were old. Yet meteorites are only found in recent layers near the earth's surface; they are never found in older layers. (See *Handy Dandy Evolution Refuter*, Robert E. Kofahl, © 1977, Beta Books, San Diego, CA, p. 123.)

Most meteorites contain large amounts of iron, and iron rusts. A buried nail can turn into a lump of rust in just a few years; an iron cannon on a sunken sailing ship becomes nearly unrecognizable after a few hundred years. There are other rarer types of meteorites which do not contain as much iron, but they are extremely fragile; they weather away very quickly. In either case, we would not expect the preservation of easily identifiable meteorites to be a common event. To complicate this further, there are lots of rusty lumps in the geologic column which are not rusted-out meteorites. We can tell whether or not a rusty lump is meteoritic in origin by laboratory analysis of the lump's elements (meteorites contain more nickel and iridium). Meteorites are valuable, but they are too rare to hunt for by digging for them; it's much more cost effective to pick up visually identifiable ones from the earth's surface—or to hunt through the rubble at the foot of a glacier. This means most of the discovered meteorites are fairly recent, but *a few have been identified* deep in the geologic column. There are two from the Ordovician period—about 450 million years ago. (See *Rocks from Space*, O. Richard Norton, © 1994, Mountain Press Publishing Company, P.O. Box 2399, Missoula, MT 59806, p. 168.)

(9) Scientists use circular reasoning to assign dates to the geologic layers and the fossils which they contain— dating each by the other.

This certainly was a problem before the development of radioactive-dating techniques, though it is not really much of a problem today. However, scientists are human and may, even today, occasionally fall into this trap. According to proper procedure, rocks are not dated by fossils unless that type of fossil has first been consistently tied to a single radioactive-date range. This is not circular reasoning. (For a valid, although controversial, application of index fossils, as these fossils are called, see *Lucy: The Beginnings of Humankind*, Donald Johanson and Maitland Edey, © 1981, Warner Books, New York, p. 238.)

> (10) The earth's magnetic field is steadily decaying; it would have been too intense in the past if the earth is old. (See *Origin and Destiny of the Earth's Magnetic Field*, Dr. Thomas G. Barnes, 1973, Institute for Creation Research, San Diego, CA.)

The evidence shows that, over the long term, the earth's magnetic field is not decaying; in fact it periodically reverses direction. This would be impossible with a simple decay phenomenon. (See *Palaeomagnetism, Principles and Applications in Geology, Geophysics and Archaeology*, D.H. Tarling, © 1983, Chapman and Hall, London, pp. 181-187.) Also, tree rings keep running records of C-14 concentrations in the atmosphere which relate to the intensity of the earth's magnetic field, but their record shows that the actual variation in C-14 concentrations since 7,000 years ago disagrees radically with what this young-earth theory predicts. (See "Carbon 14 and the Prehistory of Europe," Colin Renfrew, *Scientific American*, October 1971, vol. 225, no. 4, pp. 66,67.) A more recent version of this argument attempts to take the reversals into account. (See "The Earth's Magnetic Field Is Young," Russell Humphreys, Ph.D., Impact No. 242, *Acts & Facts*, August 1993, vol. 22, no. 8, Institute for Creation Research, El Cajon, CA 92021.) However, its young-earth conclusion is based on the *theory* that the earth's magnetic field has always lost energy at a rapid rate. That theory, in turn, depends upon the *assumption* that the fluid flow in the earth's conducting outer core does not replace this energy. The problem with this is that even simple arrangements of moving conductors have been shown to generate and maintain magnetic field energy. (See *Physics of the Earth*, Frank D. Stacey, © 1969, John Wiley and Sons, Inc., New York, pp. 154,155.)

(11) There are fossilized tree trunks cutting across many sedimentary layers which supposedly took millions of years to lay down. These fossils must have been buried quickly by a flood. (See *It's a Young World After All, Exciting Evidences for Recent Creation*, Paul D. Ackerman, © 1986, Baker Book House, Grand Rapids, MI 49506, pp. 83,84.)

In the first place, sedimentary layers do not necessarily take millions of years to deposit, nor do scientists believe they do. The layers in the Green River Formation, for example, were each produced in a single year (although the whole formation certainly took millions of years). For another example, each layer in a floodplain deposit is the result of a single flood event. Floods can come in fairly rapid succession and deposit a large amount of sediment very quickly. Although young-earth creationists often talk as if they were the only people who believe in floods, they are not. All scientists believe in many big and little floods. Noah's flood left sediments, but so did many other floods. Polystrate fossils were not all the result of Noah's flood; in fact, most were the result of other prehistoric floods or rapid sedimentation events.

(12) Rivers constantly wash minerals into the oceans; there is too little salt and other minerals in the oceans if the earth is old. (See *Scientific Creationism*, ed. Henry M. Morris, Ph.D., © 1974, Master Books, El Cajon, CA, pp. 153-155.)

This argument considers influx rates only. It ignores many aspects of the ocean's chemistry which remove minerals (for example, precipitation, strong sorption process, and nodule formation) and also ignores the fact that plate motion periodically sweeps the sea floor clear. If this argument were valid, the amount of aluminum in the ocean would prove that the earth was only 100 years old. But, of course, this argument is not valid. Ocean water does not simply result from concentration of inflowing river waters. (See *Marine Chemistry*, R.A. Horne, © 1969, Wiley-Interscience, New York, p. 424; *Continents in Collision*, Russell Miller, © 1983, Time-Life Books, Alexandria, VA, pp. 80-82; and *The Cambridge Encyclopedia of Earth Sciences*, ed. David G. Smith, Ph.D., © 1981, Crown Publishers Inc./Cambridge University Press, New York, p. 60.) A more recent version of this argument makes an attempt to evaluate removal processes as well. (See "The Sea's Missing Salt: A Dilemma for Evolutionists," Steven A. Austin, Ph.D., and D. Russell Humphreys, Ph.D., Proceedings of the Second International Conference on Creationism, July 30 through August 4, 1990, vol. II, Technical Symposium Sessions and Additional Topics, Creation Science Fellowship, Inc., 362 Ashland Ave., Pittsburgh, PA 15228, pp. 17-33.) However, excessive assumptions for groundwater additions (item A10, pp. 20-21),[50] overly optimistic assumptions about statistical precision,[51] and other errors easily make up the entire discrepancy which is claimed.

> (13) At the Paluxy River near Glen Rose, Texas, footprints of dinosaurs and humans are found together. This would not be possible under the old-earth chronology. (See *The Genesis Flood, The Biblical Record and Its Scientific Implications*, John C. Whitcomb, Th.D. and Henry M. Morris, Ph.D., © 1961, The Presbyterian and Reformed Publishing Company, pp. 173-175.)

This argument has been abandoned by most young-earth creationists. The dinosaur footprints are authentic but the "human" prints are depressions with merely superficial resemblance—like shapes seen in cloud formations. One series turned out to be misinterpreted, partial footprints of a dinosaur. (See "Defeat for Strict Creationists," Michael B. Lemonick, *Time,* June 30, 1986, vol. 127, no. 26, p. 75.) Other "human" prints have been actual forgeries—or else depressions which originally resembled a human footprint slightly, but were carved to enhance that appearance. Cross-sectional examination reveals which parts of a "fossil" impression have been carved.

Conclusions

Although it is freely admitted that there are a great many questions for which scientists have not yet produced convincing answers, the question of whether or not the earth is young is certainly *not* one of them. God's creation consistently bears witness of its old age. The evidence repeatedly confirms (within normal experimental limitations) the very old dates for the various events of the earth's history.

Is it an absolute *fact* that the earth is old? Not according to the tightly constrained definition of the term "fact" I have used in this book, but I think it's safe to say that scientists are at least as confident that the earth is old as they are that a frog hears with its ears instead of its legs. It's not the sort of proposition a wise man would choose to bet against—especially if that wise man knows he is going to stand before God to give an account of what he has taught others.

On the other hand, we have not seen a single young-earth argument which actually proved what it claimed to prove. There have been oversights or mistakes in every one of them. The young-earth *theory* simply does not agree with the creation's evidence.* This is not a situation where there are two different but equally valid ways of viewing the same evidence.

---

* Incidentally, these refuted examples prove that the claims of creationists can be "falsified" (proven wrong) in the same sense that any other scientific theory can be. This refutes the assertion sometimes made by non-creationists that creationists' claims cannot be falsified and are therefore not to be considered "scientific" theories. For example, see Hen's Teeth and Horse's Toes, Stephen Jay Gould, © 1983, W. W. Norton & Company, New York, p. 256. In this sense, creationist's theories can be considered to be scientific, but, in any case, the young-earth theories are certainly wrong.

In example after example, as we have seen, the young-earth arguments (both biblical and scientific) are simply *errors*. The choice is between one theory that is strongly confirmed by the universe's evidence and another whose "support" consists of no more than a collection of errors. If there is a valid young-earth argument, I have not encountered it during the years I have been researching this subject.

Because so many different arguments have been given, they cannot *all* be systematically refuted here. I hope if you are still unconvinced the earth is old, you will be like the Bereans of Acts 17:11 and will examine the evidence for yourself. There are plenty of libraries full of data which are free for the using.

6

The Origins of "Scientific Creationism"

> Sir, didn't you sow good seed in your field? Where then did the weeds come from?
>
> —MATTHEW 13:27

As the evidence in the preceding chapters clearly shows, the earth really is old. This raises the question of where the young-earth teaching originated. In this chapter we will attempt to answer that question by investigating the history of the controversy concerning the length and meaning of the "days" in Genesis.

Early Writers

It may come as a surprise to some readers that the Genesis-day controversy did not begin with the recent scientific determination of the earth's age but has been with us for thousands of years. During the early centuries of the church age, various prominent Christian and Jewish writers had already taken very different positions on the subject.

The Jewish historian Flavius Josephus (A.D. 37–103),[1] for example, appears to have noticed a problem with the length of the first day of creation; he also claimed to have a solution to the problem. In book I, chapter 1, verse 1, of his *Antiquities of the Jews*, he explains:

> ... and he named the beginning of light and the time of rest, *The Evening* and *The Morning*; and this was indeed the first day: but Moses said it was one day,— the cause of which I am able to give even now; but because I have promised to give such reasons for all things in a treatise by itself, I shall put off its exposition till that time.[2]

Unfortunately, Josephus never kept his promise to return to this subject—so we don't know what his solution was. It might have been interesting to examine here.

Philo (c. 20 B.C.–A.D. 45), another Jewish writer, believed that all of the creation days occurred simultaneously—that they did not take place in a space of time at all.[3] Both Justin Martyr (c. A.D. 100–166) and Irenaeus (c. A.D. 130–200) held that the days were each 1,000 years in length; this appears to have been based on their understanding that Adam died in the "day" he sinned (Genesis 2:17), that Adam lived 930 years (Genesis 5:5), and that to the Lord a thousand years is like a day (Psalm 90:4 and 2 Peter 3:8).[4] Origen (c. A.D. 185–254) argued that God's seventh day is even longer than 1,000 years—that we are still living in it.[5] St. Augustine (A.D. 354–430), on the other hand, held that the days weren't literal periods of time at all, but referred to a sequence of spiritual events.[6]

I am not claiming that the 24-hour understanding was *unknown* to the early church fathers, but it was certainly not the only position they held. In fact the 24-hour view was expressed by only a minority of the early writers. It is *not* true, as it is commonly assumed, that the 24-hour understanding was the dominant position taken by those who studied the Bible prior to the scientific influence. For readers who would like to know more about the positions of various early writers, I recommend Hugh Ross's *Creation and Time*.[7]

Since even the early church fathers were not agreed on the length of the days of Genesis, we must conclude that no one interpretation of the Genesis days is more obvious than the others. We should not be too surprised that there is still some controversy concerning this question today. At least we should not be surprised if the scientific evidence provided by God's creation had not already answered the question for us. The ancients, who lacked this evidence, could honestly question the length of the Genesis days—but why does the controversy still persist today? To answer this question, we need to take a look at some recent history.

Changes in Science

When the scientific evidence for the great age of the earth first started becoming available in the late 1700s, the church had no great difficulty accepting the old-earth position. In fact, the scientific theory that the earth was very old was originally proposed by a Christian creationist named James Hutton. Hutton believed God had created the world and would eventually destroy it, but he also believed that God's creation was very durable and self-repairing—not one which was wearing out on its own.[8]

The church was just becoming comfortable with the scientific dates when something happened that threw a monkey wrench into the works: Darwin published his theory of evolution. Darwin's theory would not have caused so much trouble if it hadn't actually seemed to fit some of the emerging evidence. Because the theory offered the world a plausible naturalistic explanation for biological origins, it had immense appeal to those who wanted to remove God from their thinking.

Some Christians, although they had no need or desire to eliminate God, thought Darwin's theory was plausible anyway and attempted to harmonize it with their theology.[9] Other

Christians rejected evolution altogether. As more scientists began accepting evolution, those Christians who stood against Darwin found themselves less and less willing to accept the authority of the scientific establishment. As a result it became increasingly popular to ignore the opinions of the scientists altogether. Unfortunately, this meant the scientific evidence from God's creation also tended to be ignored.

Ellen G. White

At about this time, a new group emerged, presently known as the Seventh-Day Adventists, who had their own reasons for breaking with traditional science. Leading this group, in practice if not title, was their prophetess, Ellen G. White, whose visions were, at that time, taken by her followers as being equal in authority with the Bible.

As the Adventists came to learn over the years, placing this much faith in a human leader can cause trouble. Differences between White's writings and the Bible eventually led to problems in church management. When this happened, the Adventists wisely chose to resolve the problems by dropping White's writings as a source of doctrinal authority[10]— although they are still regarded today with very high respect.

This bit of religious history is relevant to the present discussion because the currently popular form of young-earth creationism is a consequence and outgrowth of Ellen G. White's visions of the creation event. In particular, strict insistence on 24-hour creation days, flood geology, and many specific "scriptural" arguments have their roots in White's visions. Consider the following quotation from her 1864 publication, *Facts of Faith.*

> I was then carried back to the creation and was shown that the first week, in which God performed the work of creation in six days and rested on the seventh day, was just like every other week. The great God in his days of creation and day of rest, measured off the first cycle as a sample for successive weeks till the close of

time. . . . The weekly cycle of seven literal days, six for labor, and the seventh for rest, which has been preserved and brought down through Bible history, originated in the great facts of the first seven days.

When God spake his law with an audible voice from Sinai, he introduced the Sabbath by saying, "Remember the Sabbath day to keep it holy." . . . He then, in giving the reason for thus observing the week, points them back to his example on the first seven days of time. "For in six days the Lord made heaven and earth, the sea and all that in them is, and rested the seventh day, wherefore the Lord blessed the Sabbath day and hallowed it." This reason appears beautiful and forcible when we understand the record of creation to mean literal days. . . .

But the infidel supposition, that the events of the first week required seven vast, indefinite periods for their accomplishment, strikes directly at the foundation of the Sabbath of the fourth commandment. It makes indefinite and obscure that which God has made very plain. . . .[11]

It is worth noting that some parts of this vision—and not just the parts which are quotations of Scripture—sound strangely familiar today. Parts of this argument are still often repeated, essentially unchanged, by present-day young-earth creationists. Why this is so will become apparent below, but first we will examine more of White's visions. The reason short, 24-hour creation days were important to White can be seen from another of her visions:

He [Satan] then led on his representatives to attempt to change the fourth, or Sabbath, commandment, thus altering the only one of the ten which brings to view the true God, the Maker of the heavens and the earth. Satan presented before them the glorious resurrection of Jesus, and told them that by His rising on the first day of the week, He changed the Sabbath from the seventh to the first day of the week.

> . . . I was shown that the law of God would stand fast forever . . . I saw that the Sabbath never will be done away; but that the redeemed saints, and all the angelic host, will observe it in honor of the great Creator to all eternity.[12]

Here we see that White considered the seventh-day observance of the fourth commandment to stand apart from the others in importance. She considered "literal" 24-hour creation "days" to be important because they supported the literal observance of the seventh-day Sabbath. Those who kept God's rest on Sunday were, in her view, following Satan's lead in violation of God's eternal pattern. The idea that the creation days were longer than 24 hours was incompatible with her belief that the human Sabbath cycles must be eternally synchronized with God's.

Price's New Geology

Because White's early followers regarded her visions as being equal in authority with the Bible, they believed the creation days had to be 24 hours long. One of these followers, George McCready Price had some scientific training.[13] When he began encountering geological evidence for the antiquity of the earth, he realized he had a problem. After some searching, he found what he believed to be the solution in another of White's visions:[14]

> [After the flood] The beautiful, regular shaped mountains had disappeared. Stones, ledges, and ragged rocks appeared upon some parts of the earth which were before out of sight. Where had been hills and mountains, no traces of them were visible. . . .

> Before the flood there were immense forests. The trees were many times larger than any trees which we now see. . . . At the time of the flood these forests were torn up or broken down and buried in the earth. In some places large quantities of these immense trees were thrown together and covered with stones and

earth by the commotions of the flood. They have since petrified and become coal, which accounts for the large coal beds which are now found. This coal has produced oil. . . .[15]

White claimed that Noah's flood had caused a great deal of geological commotion. Price reasoned that if *all* of the geological evidence for an old earth could be explained by this commotion, then he did not need to abandon White's 24-hour creation days. So Price took on the immense task of rewriting the entire science of geology to conform it to White's visions of the creation and the flood.

Because evidence for an old earth is found throughout the geological record, Price had to attribute most of it to Noah's flood. This meant Price had to come up with a flood-related explanation for nearly everything found in the earth. For example, Price took White's vision of coal resulting from immense forests buried by Noah's flood, and reworked it into something sounding more like geological science than a religious vision. This involved comparing his flood-geology theory with competing theories—including the standard theory that coal results from peat bogs. After presenting the other theories and briefly discussing their difficulties, Price provided his own as "The Probable Method":

The Probable Method of the Formation of the Coal Beds. If we care to go into the question of probabilities, and can picture to ourselves a wide stretch of country clothed for long periods with a most luxuriant vegetation, and if we may suppose that the remarkable atmospheric conditions of the ancient world may have absolutely precluded any parching drought, thus rendering it quite improbable that the accumulated deposits of centuries should ever be burned up by forest fires, we shall have the probable *source of the materials.* If now, in the great world catastrophe which seems to be indicated, these accumulations of many centuries were all washed away, dead and green together, and swept pell-mell into lakes or valleys,

> somewhat like the great natural "raft" on the Red
> River, only on a far more enormous scale, the stumps
> of the trees would still carry many of their roots with
> them, and would frequently float in the natural or
> upright position....[16]

Price was aware of trees in coal formations, roots down, as if they had simply grown in that position. The standard peat-bog theory of coal formation naturally allowed for this. In answer, Price envisioned the trees being swept into place, floating vertically or possibly even held in this position by a surrounding "raft" of organic matter. Instead of a tranquil, lakelike environment for Noah's flood, Price envisioned something more like rushing "rivers" which could transport the entire material of huge forests into concentrated piles, which later would be turned into coal.

Price's reworkings of White's visions also required a little bit of hedging in a few places. Although he adopted her notion that coal produced oil (coal and oil do not necessarily even occur in the same parts of the world),[17] he also allowed that oil could be produced from other organic materials. As Price put it:

> Mineral *oil* and mineral *gas* contain only carbon and
> hydrogen. Both were probably formed by distillation
> from coal beds, and other organic deposits.[18]

This was the beginning of flood geology, and of what later grew into the modern form of young-earth creationism. Price devoted his life to promoting flood geology and wrote many books on the subject. Because many Christians were, at this time, looking for answers to the threat posed by Darwin's theory, and because they had lost faith in the scientific establishment, Price's writings drew quite a bit of attention. For a brief period his writings even achieved some acceptance outside of Adventist circles, but Price's lack of academic credentials and his Adventist flavor greatly limited his success.

Modern Creation Science

Although Price did not have the proper credentials to gain popular acceptance, his writings eventually attracted the attention of two men who did. John C. Whitcomb, Th.D., and Henry M. Morris, Ph.D., became interested in Price's ideas, cleaned them up a little, and incorporated them in their book *The Genesis Flood, the Biblical Record and Its Scientific Implications*.[19] The part of their book which dealt with scientific evidence was the work of Henry Morris. When Morris needed an explanation for the formation of coal, he had one essentially ready to go in Price's writings. The connection between Price's and Morris's descriptions is not explicit, but it is still easily visible. As Morris explained in *The Genesis Flood*:

> The physical evidence plainly and emphatically demonstrates the fact that the coal seams are water-laid deposits, in which great agglomerations of plants were rafted down on the surface of the Deluge rivers, then conveyed back and forth on the shifting currents until finally brought to rest in some basin of deposition, to be followed by a reacting current from another direction bearing non-organic materials perhaps, then another current with a load of plant debris, and so on. The only evidence cited in favor of the peat-bog theory of coal formation, such as the upright trunks, the stigmaria, etc., can, as we have seen, equally well or better be interpreted as resulting from the nature of the rafts of vegetation being floated into their final place of deposition by flood waters.[20]

When explaining oil formation, Morris would naturally have been influenced by Price's theory that oil formed not directly, but "by distillation from coal beds, and other organic deposits." Although Morris did his own research, he appears to have been sufficiently influenced that he settled on a theory which, as he put it, "may not stand the test of further investigation." Although he realized he was sticking his neck out, the theory he selected for his book carried the essence of Price's indirect "distillation" from other sources:

> Thus, it would seem that crude oil originates during the compaction of a sedimentary basin by virtue of the fact that sediment hydrocarbons dissolve in waters containing natural solubilizers and then come out of solution as oil droplets. . . .

> This process of oil formation implies, too, that oil was formed over wide areas, rather than in the relatively limited locations in which it is found. . . .

> This hypothesis is quite new and may not stand the test of further investigation, but it is based on an impressive research study. In any case, the general picture of vast organic remains, somehow dissolved and transformed chemically into petroleum hydrocarbons, then eventually reprecipitated as oil, is basically valid and harmonizes well with the concept of catastrophic burial and dissolution during the Deluge.[21]

What starts to become apparent here is that modern flood geology is not, as we might have assumed, the result of careful, literal Bible reading combined with scientific study. Instead, the picture which emerges is that modern flood geology has been heavily influenced by White's visions. When Morris says his presentation "harmonizes well with the concept of catastrophic burial and dissolution during the Deluge," this is not so much a harmonization with Scripture as with Ellen G. White's theology.

The connection to Price and the Adventists worried Whitcomb and Morris. Unfortunately their actions reflected more concern with the outward appearance than with the substance. Fearing that Price's Adventist-tinted reputation might hinder acceptance of *The Genesis Flood*, Whitcomb and Morris tried to avoid any visible connection with Price. Although they left the substance of their arguments unchanged, they removed nearly every mention of Price's name from their book. This irritated many of Price's friends who felt Whitcomb and Morris had not given him sufficient credit for the intellectual debt they owed him.[22] One of the few remaining references to Price is found on page 184 of *The Genesis Flood*:

> Long ago, George McCready Price made an extensive study of areas of this type [overthrust faults] around the world. He discussed these in many books written by him on the general theme of deluge geology. Although his examples were very impressive and well-documented, his writings were largely ignored by geologists, ostensibly because of his largely self-made geologic education.

Another reference to Price is found on page 211:

> Had the above charges been made by George McCready Price or some other modern opponent of uniformitarian geology, they would have been indignantly discounted as the rantings of an ignorant fundamentalist!

These references reveal the concern that Whitcomb and Morris felt about associating themselves too closely with Price. But although they carefully avoided the outward appearance of connection, the actual fact remains visible. *The Genesis Flood*, as it has been variously described, is essentially an "updated version" of Price's *New Geology* or a "reissue of G.M. Price's views brought up to date."[23]

Of course there is nothing wrong with using an old idea *if* that idea is the truth. Real truth lasts forever. Unfortunately, the central claim of flood geology—that most of the fossil-bearing strata (including all of the Mesozoic layers) were deposited during Noah's flood[24]—is simply false. This can be seen by examining a formation called The Grand Staircase which straddles the Utah-Arizona border.[25] The Grand Staircase is so large that the Grand Canyon is a mere ditch which runs through its foot. In the middle of this huge sequence of layers is a 2,000-foot-thick layer called the Navajo Sandstone.[26] This layer of cross-bedded sandstone makes up most of the cliffs of Zion National Park, in Utah. Why this layer is interesting to us is that it was deposited in a *dry* environment by winds and shifting sand-dunes.[27] This wind-deposited layer sits right in the middle of the Mesozoic layers which, according to flood geology, were supposedly deposited during Noah's flood. Although Noah's flood was a real, historic event, it simply cannot be used to explain all of the geological evidence for an old earth; the truth is most of the earth's geology had formed long before the time of Noah's flood.

Anyone can make a mistake, but it seems that once a mistake has been made it can take on a life of its own. It can keep on spreading. The currently popular version of young-earth creationism—with its 24-hour days and flood geology—began with the visions of Ellen G. White, was reworked by George McCready Price into a scientific format, and was ultimately appropriated by Dr. Henry M. Morris—possibly the man most connected with young-earth creationism. Most people are aware of the subsequent explosive growth and popularity of the teaching among evangelical Christians following the publication of *The Genesis Flood*. If any readers are interested in detailed information on the history and growth of "scientific creationism" the book *The Creationists, the Evolution of Scientific Creation,* by Ronald L. Numbers, is recommended.[28]

Conclusions

We are reminded again of the "lion and the lamb" at the beginning of this book, and how we humans seem to confuse what we have repeatedly heard with God's holy truth. Henry Morris, no less than the rest of us, appears to have succumbed to this. He appears to have confused what he heard through George McCready Price with what the Bible really says about the creation and Noah's flood. His rigorous adherence to what the Bible teaches appears to be, in effect, merely a rigorous adherence to what Ellen G. White believed the Bible taught. Paul's advice in 1 Thessalonians 5:21 that we "test everything" is extremely important and needs continuous application. Otherwise mere humans seem to be destined to follow the wrong paths. The truth is a very narrow path; those who do not pay close attention are not likely to stay on it for long.

God's written Word is completely without errors, but humans—even great Christian leaders—are prone to error. This was true of the early church fathers, who took every conceivable position concerning the meaning of the days of Genesis. It is also true of the founders of every subsequent denomination and teaching. The same truth continually recurs: Christian leaders—even those regarded by their followers as having the gift of prophecy—are humans and humans sometimes make mistakes.

7

Understanding Genesis Chapter One

By wisdom the LORD laid the earth's foundations, by
understanding he set the heavens in place; by his
knowledge the deeps were divided, and the clouds let
drop the dew.

—PROVERBS 3:19,20

The "days" of the first chapter of Genesis certainly allow
for a very old universe, but Genesis 1 brings up many other
questions which must also be answered; we still need to see if
the old-earth understanding can answer these questions. Here
the various statements made in Genesis 1 will be examined in
the combined light of what the Bible says and what scientists
have been able to learn about God's creation.

As will be seen, the rocks and stars are rich in very detailed
information; they say a great deal about their origin and their
Creator. Unfortunately, the Bible contains very few total pages
about the origin of the universe, and what it does relate is
much less detailed than we might like. While it will not necessarily be easy to decipher what either account is telling us,
neither source should ever be disregarded. Often we will find
the answers to our questions in God's Bible, but there will be
times when we will find more detailed answers in His creation.

This chapter presents some *theories* which attempt to correlate Genesis 1 with the universe. These theories are certainly not the final word, they are merely possibilities which were designed to fit the evidence. Scientific *evidence* can occasionally expose an incorrect *theory* about Scripture, but it can never prove that any theory is correct.

Genesis 1 will be examined very closely. Where it is scientifically possible, we will examine *how* God worked in addition to *what* He did. Although at times God left the scientists without a clue as to how He worked, at other times He left so much evidence of His methodology that a determined atheist can imagine that the processes could have occurred even without God's hand on them. As God's Bible reflects the individual styles of its many human recorders, so also His universe retains the marks of His various channels of creation—sometimes supernatural,* other times quite natural.** In all cases, in both God's Bible and in His universe, we see God's wisdom revealed through the ultimate result.

Creationists often emphasize God's power and authority and neglect His wisdom, knowledge, and understanding. As Proverbs 3:19,20 (quoted at the beginning of this chapter) tells us, these three played an important role in the creation. We often erroneously picture God as a sort of powerful magician who speaks a single magic word, then steps back and watches while the heavens obey. According to this image, God does not reason out each of the incomprehensible myriad details of what He is doing. The actual working out of those minute elements of design is somehow left up to the "magic" itself, but of course, God *is* the "magic." It is He who works out every microscopic detail.

---

* For example, the cosmic explosion which scientists call the "Big Bang."

** For example, the building up of the present composition of the earth's atmosphere.

Psalm 33:6 states: "By the word of the LORD were the heavens made."[1] Here God's creative agency is metaphorically described as the "word." (In John 1:1, Jesus is similarly described as the "Word.") Psalm 33:9 continues, "For he spoke, and it came to be; he commanded, and it stood firm." Once God has spoken something, it is certainly as good as done, but this is different from saying that God merely spoke the command, then sat back and watched some other creative agency deliver the results. God created the universe by Himself (Isaiah 44:24). God does have the power to "speak things into existence," but we must remember that He also *is* that power. He is the one who does, as well as the one who speaks. God worked out every single detail Himself. He "made the earth by his power," but He also "founded the world by his wisdom" (Jeremiah 10:12,51:15).

God once gave Job a brief and highly figurative lecture on how much attention to detail was required to create the universe:

> Where were you when I laid the earth's foundation? Tell me, if you understand. Who marked off its dimensions? Surely you know! Who stretched a measuring line across it? On what were its footings set, or who laid its cornerstone—while the morning stars sang together and all the angels shouted for joy? . . .
>
> —JOB 38:4-7

Today, scientists are able to read some of these details. Like Job, we can never really appreciate just how much was involved in making the universe, but what we can learn from science will help us to better understand how awesome God really is.

DAY 1
THE UNIVERSE

Genesis 1:1

In the beginning God created the heavens and
the earth.

As recently as the early 1900s, it was taught in physics
courses that matter could neither be created nor destroyed. If
matter could not be created, then it must always have existed
and there never would have been a beginning. Christians
would have known better, but they would have had no scientific support for their belief.

Modern physics now confirms what Bible-believing Christians knew by faith all along. Einstein supplied the necessary
relationship between matter and energy[2] and later the
Heisenberg uncertainty principle supplied a possible relation
between energy and time. Scientists are now quite willing to
concede that a moment of creation was possible. Other evidence even dictates the *necessity* of a creation. The famous
second law of thermodynamics (Boltzmann/Kelvin) establishes that the universe must not have always existed or it
would have run down to a dead stop before now.[3]

Hubble's correlation between red shifts and distances to
stars, and the consequent rate of expansion for the universe,
even indicates a rough estimate for the time of the creation.[4] As
Hubble's observations showed, the more distant galaxies have
proportionally greater red shifts. (Red shift is a measure of how
rapidly a distant galaxy is traveling away from us.) Mathematically, this means that all galaxies are moving away from a single
point in space and that they all must have started from there at
the same time. All of the matter in the universe is behaving as if
it were the debris left over from a colossal explosion which once
happened at that point. Using his limited information, Hubble
calculated that this explosion must have occurred about 2 billion

years ago.[5] Later refinements corrected this very rough first estimate to the presently accepted range of 10 to 20 billion years.

Penzias and Wilson's measurement of the universe's background radiation confirms a very violent beginning at about
this time.[6] More recently, evidence from nucleosynthesis[7] has
quantitatively confirmed some of the fine detail concerning
this event which cosmologists call the "big bang."

Although correct in substance, the big bang theory is often
couched in terminology which assumes atheism. This, unfortunately, makes Christians reject it without even considering it
logically. An atheist will attempt to present the moment of creation as if it were a completely random accident—one which,
by lucky coincidence, started a chain reaction of cause and
effect that ultimately fell together into the Sistine Chapel and
Marilyn Monroe among other wonders. But the "big bang"
requires neither unguided randomness nor an accident.
Besides, even those processes which appear random to humans
are under God's control. "The lot is cast into the lap, but its
every decision is from the LORD" (Proverbs 16:33).*

Design and purpose in the guiding hand of an intelligent
creator are consistent with the evidence for this cosmic-scaled
explosion, but the random-accident scenario leaves an endless list of unanswered questions: How was the wildly
expanding fireball sculpted into the universe's galaxies? How
was the immense gravitational attraction of all this tightly concentrated mass overcome?** And what could possibly have set
it off in the first place?[8]

In any case, the moment of creation has been conceded.
Modern science has come as far as giving us a description of how
the universe began which even matches the details of the biblical
account. According to Einstein's laws, before there was any

---

* This is also the theme of the entire book of Esther.

** Under Einstein's laws, the gravitational attraction would have been so intense
that time itself would be unable to proceed in a "real" forward direction! Perhaps new scientific discoveries will eventually throw light on these questions.

energy or matter in the universe, there could not have been any time or space either.[9] If there was no time "before" this event, then there really was no "before" at all! Although this confuses us, it is not a problem for God; His existence is somehow independent of time as it relates to our physical universe.

Time and space cannot exist where there is no matter. This means that the moment of the creation of matter marked the beginning of time and the creation of the "heavens" which we call "space." This sounds very similar to the Bible's "In the beginning God created the heavens and the earth" (Genesis 1:1). The similarity becomes complete when we examine the different possible meanings for the Hebrew word "erets" (translated "earth" here). According to Gesenius' lexicon, "erets" carried the alternate meaning "element of the earth" to the ancient Hebrews.[10] This means the word "earth" in this verse could refer to cosmic matter in the general sense—the matter from which the earth, stars, and planets were ultimately formed. With this understanding, the biblical and scientific accounts of the first moment of creation match exactly! In the beginning (time created) God created the heavens (space) and the earth (cosmic matter).

Cosmologists tell us that about 10 or 20 billion years ago, matter, time, and space appeared together with the cosmic "big bang." The energy of this explosion was what caused the creation of the cosmic matter and sent it spreading in all directions at nearly the speed of light. According to relativity, even "space" itself spreads with the mass of the stars.[11] Notice how this account matches with Jeremiah 10:12: "God made the earth by his power; he founded the world by his wisdom and stretched out the heavens by his understanding." In particular, notice the cause-and-effect connection between matter and energy* and how the

---

* Even if we were to insist on technical accuracy and differentiate between "energy" and "power" we would have no trouble here because energy is equivalent to power operating for some period of time. But, of course, it would be silly for us to insist that ancient Hebrew prophets respect present-day technical distinctions in their writings.

heavens are spread out. The word "earth" is again translated from "erets" and may again refer to matter in general.

Although in the past science did not seem to bear out Genesis 1:1, at the present time it bears it out very closely— just so long as we are willing to accept a longer-than-24-hour interpretation for the creative "days." Scientists now tell us that matter was created under exactly the circumstances which the Bible described thousands of years ago. Of course the scientists have not yet been able to fathom every aspect of God's creation, but they have come a long way.

This confirms some observations made back in the second chapter of this book: Even if *science* disagrees with *theology*, that does not necessarily prove that theology is in error. As we know today, theologians of the last century were correct in saying that the universe was created—even when this was still in disagreement with science. Similarly, even if theology appears to be in agreement with science, that does not necessarily prove that we are interpreting the Bible correctly. Interpreters of both Scripture and the universe can be wrong at the same time—even when they agree with each other.* Remember that the Inquisition used both Scripture and science against Galileo! Truth can be very elusive, no simple approach can always be trusted to lead us in the correct direction.

Genesis 1:2

Now the earth was formless and empty, darkness was over the surface of the deep, and the Spirit of God was hovering over the waters.

This is also a very interesting verse and a subject of much controversy. Creationists sometimes place a huge time gap

---

* It, of course, follows that my attempts to correlate present-day scientific theories with the Bible should not be taken too seriously. If science moves on, this book will suffer the same fate as many other past attempts to correlate the Bible with the teachings of men. The only reason I have bothered to write it at all is that I am convinced that the scientists have finally stumbled onto some actual truth. Time will judge.

here in which many things supposedly happened which were not recorded in the Bible. This theory was originally proposed as an attempt to correlate the purported short days of Genesis with the long ones of science. It adds a complication to scriptural interpretation which is totally unnecessary; the "days" of Genesis can refer to long periods of time without the need for invented gaps. Such complications should always be avoided when there is neither a scientific nor biblical reason for them.*

In Genesis 1:1, God created the matter from which the planet earth was later to be formed. Here in verse two, the description of this matter progresses. If we take Genesis 1:2 as a literal description of how our solar system (the earth, sun, moon, and planets) actually looked as it was being formed, this yields good agreement with modern scientific theory concerning this event. If instead verse two is taken to describe just the early earth, immediately *following* the formation of our solar system, there is still good agreement with scientific theory. Because both the biblical and scientific data concerning this event are so vague, there is a lot of room for speculation. Some possibilities will be suggested here.

There are many theories concerning the formation of our solar system and much is still unknown. However, astronomers agree that solar systems form from clouds of interstellar matter called nebulae.[12] A nebula is a very large, shapeless cloud of interstellar gas and dust (cosmic matter) floating in space. In the case of the formation of our own solar system, this cloud is believed to have contained the remains of an ancient star (or stars) which exploded long ago.[13] Eventually, gravitational forces pulled this matter into clumps which became our sun and its planets. At first, before the sun ignited, this process took place in the darkness of interstellar space.

---

* Although it would be an unnecessary digression from the subject to comment on this theory here, my opinions are included in Appendix 4 for anyone who is interested.

This scientific reckoning of the formation of our solar system (from a dark, shapeless cloud of space dust) bears a remarkable resemblance to the Bible's "the earth was formless and empty, darkness was over the surface of the deep." The word "earth" was again translated from "erets" and could therefore refer to the drifting matter of a dark nebula. But there is no reason why this verse could not refer to just the incompletely formed planet earth which was still in darkness—either because the dark cloud of dust still enveloped it or because the sun had not yet ignited.

Continuing in the second verse, "The Spirit of God was hovering over the waters." This is also very rich in possible interpretations. Here emphasis is shifted from "matter" in general to "water" more specifically; this appears to be accompanied by a shift in focus to the surface of the newly formed planet where most of the remainder of God's creative activity is to occur. Water is the focus of the next few verses, and the planet's surface is where this water resides.

The phrase "was hovering" ("moved" in the KJV) is translated from the Hebrew "rachaph" which is used only two other places in the entire Bible (Deuteronomy 32:11 and Jeremiah 23:9). The word means something like "to be moved or affected" as with love or fear.[14] Jeremiah 23:9 says, ". . . My heart is broken within me; all my bones tremble. . . ." Here the word "tremble" is translated from "rachaph." In this case the one who is speaking is being moved by distress. Deuteronomy 32:11 gives a nicer picture. "Like an eagle that stirs up its nest, and hovers over its young, . . ." Here "rachaph" was translated as "hovers." (This is also how the NIV translated this word in Genesis 1:2.) This time it is used in a sense similar to a hen brooding over her eggs—being moved with love rather than fear or distress. This might be what is intended in Genesis 1:2, but as we will see, the Jeremiah usage might also be the truth. God may have intended both shades of meaning at the same time.

There are other sources of uncertainty in this verse. The word "Spirit" (translated in Genesis 1:2 from the Hebrew "ruach") could also be translated as "breath" or "wind." If "wind" were the intended meaning, then the phrase "of God" would probably take on another shade of meaning, more like "mighty" or "violent."[15] This would imply the less-gentle understanding of "rachaph" implied by Jeremiah. A mightily raging wind could certainly be described as being moved with "emotion." This phrase could be translated "and the wind of God raged on the waters." This would not necessarily mean that the "brooded" meaning implied by Deuteronomy 32:11 is wrong; if God meant to accomplish a creative step with a mighty wind, it would still represent a loving God "brooding" over His creation.

Stars such as our sun generate a "wind" of sorts. This "wind" is comprised of elementary particles which "blow" away from those stars at about a million miles per hour. A new star will sporadically flare and generate this "wind" in bursts. It is possible that the Hebrew word translated "spirit" here might refer to a great burst of solar "wind" from a giant sun flare. Scientists believe that such a blast may have cleared away much of the nebular dust.[16] Under this interpretation, the sun might already have been shining before this time, but its light would not yet be visible from earth because of an excessive amount of surrounding dust. A strong enough blast would clear this dust away. Notice that under this interpretation, we might expect light to become visible immediately following the blast of "wind."

Genesis 1:3

And God said, "Let there be light," and there was light.

As previously explained, our solar system, including the sun, the moon, the earth, and the other planets, was originally formed from nebular space dust falling together into clumps. The sun was by far the largest clump and, according to the laws of thermodynamics, would therefore be much hotter and under much more pressure than the planets were.

If you have ever had an opportunity to use an old-fashioned hand-operated tire pump, you can appreciate that air gets hotter when it is compressed. The pump can get so hot that it becomes uncomfortable to hold. The forces involved in a forming star are much greater and the temperatures thus generated are great indeed! When the material of the forming star (which is mostly hydrogen) becomes hot enough, the star will ignite[17]—quite literally as a giant, continuously burning hydrogen bomb!

When this happens, there is light. The nuclear fusion reaction takes place way down in the center of the newly formed star. Eventually its energy will reach the surface and the star will begin to shine. Genesis 1:3 may describe the creation of the sun or it may describe a time when the sun's light first became visible to the earth owing to the removal of some nebular dust. Either way, God created the sun during His first "day." As will be explained later, another event is described during God's fourth "day." Scientists date this event—the creation of the sun and planets—at about 4.5 billion years ago.

Genesis 1:4,5

> God saw that the light was good, and he separated the light from the darkness. God called the light "day," and the darkness he called "night." And there was evening and there was morning—the first day.

As was mentioned, stars generate a "wind" of sorts, and a new star will sporadically flare and generate this "wind" in bursts. After a star has settled into a stable routine, this stellar or solar "wind" also stabilizes.* The stellar wind would eventually blow the remaining dust away from the solar system, but at the moment of the star's ignition, there would still be plenty of interplanetary dust present. At first, there may have been enough to keep the planets in darkness.

With time, there would have been less dust. At some point the solar system must have merely been a hazy place; sunlight would have bounced around in a moderate amount of interplanetary dust. Hence, the first sunlight would have reached the earth from all sides. Even the back side of the earth would be illuminated by light reflected off this dust. Adding to this, the earth was initially very hot. It may have been hot enough to glow and emit some light of its own—although it never reached a high enough temperature to become a star like the sun did.[18] These initial conditions would have produced light on both sides of the earth at the same time; there would have been no night. Genesis 1:4,5 tells us that God separated the light from the darkness; the scientific account tells us He did this by further clearing of the interplanetary dust with the solar wind—and possibly by cooling the earth's surface.

From the absence of heavy inert gases in our present atmosphere, scientists conclude that the earth's original atmosphere must have been entirely stripped off. One theory is that this was done by a huge burst of the solar wind from a giant flare.[19] Possible evidence for this flare is seen in the differences between the inner and outer planets. The four inner planets (Mercury, Venus, Earth, and Mars) are all essentially bare rocks, having relatively thin atmospheres. These four may all have been within range of the solar flare and had their original thick atmospheres removed. This was actually good because those atmospheres were made of poisonous gases

---

* The Hebrew phrase "God saw that the light was good" could be translated "God saw to it that the light was good." This might mean that God had to bring the light under control before it was what he had in mind. See Gesenius' Hebrew-Chaldee Lexicon to the Old Testament, © 1979, Baker Book House Co., Grand Rapids, MI, p. 749, entry #7200, definition 2e.

anyway. The next four planets (Jupiter, Saturn, Uranus, and Neptune) are gas giants with rocky cores. Those cores are roughly comparable in size to the four inner planets.* It appears these giants were out of range of the solar flare; they still have their original atmospheres which are thousands of miles thick. Interestingly, separating the inner and outer planets, at about the suggested limit of this flare, is a cloud of debris called the asteroid belt.

A flare this powerful would have removed the earth's oceans as well as its atmosphere. Although Genesis does not specifically tell us of a time when the earth was without a surrounding shell of water,[20] it is still possible that such an event may have happened. Many things certainly happened to the early earth which are not mentioned in the Bible. The scientific evidence strongly suggests that earth was once stripped bare like the moon. This is what will be assumed here in our attempt to piece together the scriptural and scientific evidence.

In any case, the cosmic dust filling our solar system was eventually cleared away. At present, there is scarcely any dust or debris left floating in our part of space at all—just a few atoms per cubic inch and an occasional meteoroid, comet, or asteroid. When this dust finally blew away, the light from the sun hit the earth directly as it does today. This meant one side of the turning planet was bathed in the sun's light while the other side was in the earth's own shadow. When the earth's surface cooled, it could not emit light so the shadow side was truly in darkness. Hence there was the separation of the day from the night. Again, God's universe tells the same story His biblical account does.

---

* Pluto is not a gas giant, but neither is it necessarily one of the original planets. Its orbit is much more elliptical than the other eight planets (actually coming nearer to the sun than Neptune at one point); this suggests it may have been captured by the sun's gravity at some time after the other planets had formed. New information suggests that Pluto and its moon Charon are merely the two largest members of the Kuiper belt of comets; it might be more accurate to call them comets than a planet and its moon. See "Beyond Neptune," John Horgan, Scientific American, October 1995, vol. 273, no. 4, p. 24.

DAY 2
SEPARATION OF THE WATERS

Genesis 1:6-8

And God said, "Let there be an expanse between the waters to separate water from water." So God made the expanse and separated the water under the expanse from the water above it. And it was so. God called the expanse "sky." And there was evening, and there was morning—the second day.

Although the earth's original atmospheric water was removed when its first atmosphere was stripped, the makings for the present atmosphere and oceans—nitrogen, carbon dioxide, and water—were safely held (chemically bound) in the earth's rocks. With time, these elements were released by volcanic eruptions and hydrothermal activity such as geysers.[21] In the next few verses we see God working on the water of this second atmosphere.

In these verses the word "sky" is translated from the Hebrew "shamayim." Although "shamayim" is the same Hebrew word translated "heavens" in verse one, those "heavens" are different from the "sky" which God is creating here. Remember, the same word can sometimes be used to mean two different things even in the same biblical passage. In verse one, God created the heavens which we call "space." Here He is creating the heavens which we call "the sky."

As mentioned previously, the early earth was quite hot. At first it may have even reached temperatures high enough to melt rocks.[22] The center of the earth is hot enough to melt rocks even today, but it is kept heated by energy from radioactive minerals.[23] The earth's surface did cool with time, though. First the earth cooled sufficiently to form a solid crust. Later, it became cool enough that volcanic steam could condense upon it into liquid water.[24] This appears to be what is written about in verses six through eight. Instead of having one big cloud of steam (water in gas form) surrounding the planet, water condensed onto its surface (the waters below) while a great mass of clouds (the waters above) remained above the growing "expanse" of air.

We get another view of this in the book of Proverbs:

> By wisdom the Lord laid the earth's foundations, by understanding he set the heavens in place; by his knowledge the deeps were divided, and the clouds let drop the dew.
> —PROVERBS 3:19,20

This adds more detail to the division of the deeps.[25] The waters above (as identified in Genesis) are described here in Proverbs 3 as clouds which drop dew to form the waters below. Proverbs 8 also contributes to our picture of this event:

> I [wisdom] was there when he set the heavens in place, when he marked out the horizon on the face of the deep, when he established the clouds above and fixed securely the fountains of the deep, . . .
> —PROVERBS 8:27,28

As before, there is good agreement between what the Bible tells us God did and what scientific understanding tells us happened. Scientific understanding is finally converging upon the biblical account which, remarkably, was composed thousands of years ago. Of course, God was there and He knew what happened when He created the world. No one else could have known until this past century (without getting his information from God).

Although scarcely worth mentioning today, the Hebrew word "raqia," translated "expanse" in Genesis 1:6, was in times past a source of confusion. Theologians from around the time of the translation of the King James Bible (and before) seriously regarded the "expanse" as a physical dome which held liquid water up above the sky;[26] hence the translation "firmament" in the King James Version. In verses such as Genesis

7:11 where it figuratively says, "The windows of heaven were opened" (KJV), those theologians envisioned literal windows opening in the dome of the sky and spilling the waters through. That, of course, is not how God causes rain!

There was actually some justification for this historic misinterpretation. The root of "raqia" means to spread out by beating—as one might hammer out a bowl from a piece of copper.[27] One could easily understand this word to mean a sky-size inverted physical bowl which has been beaten into shape; this would be as easy as understanding the word to mean a separation or spreading. In fact, without the realization that the waters above could hold themselves aloft in the form of thick clouds, it would be much easier to imagine something physical supporting them.

Of course modern translations reflect the more scientifically correct understanding. The word "expanse" is now used instead of the less correct "firmament." There is really nothing new about scientists aiding theologians in biblical interpretation and translation; it has been going on for quite some time.

DAY 3
DRY LAND AND PLANTS

Genesis 1:9,10

And God said, "Let the water under the sky be gathered to one place, and let dry ground appear." And it was so. God called the dry ground "land," and the gathered waters he called "seas." And God saw that it was good.

When the water first condensed onto the young planet's surface, the earth was still very smooth; it was possible for the oceans to cover it entirely. This is because the earth, as a whole, actually behaves more like a liquid mass than a solid ball. Liquids will not form mountains or valleys very well.* Scientists believe that the earth actually was, at one time, completely covered by a shallow sea. At that time, the only solid matter which might occasionally have broken the water's surface would have been volcanic islands.[28]

Although scientists do not yet know exactly how it happened, geologists tell us that by 2.5 billion years ago, the more or less rigid continental masses had formed.[29] These masses, made of relatively light weight rock, floated on top of other rock which was heavier and hot enough to behave more like a liquid than a solid.[30] This is similar to how a marshmallow floats in hot chocolate or how aluminum floats in liquid mercury. In this way, the continents were able to reach above the surface of the ocean (see illustration on next page). The phrase "let the dry ground appear" seems to speak of this time when the continents first formed.

We need not be concerned that the Bible describes the waters as being gathered into one place, rather than into several different oceans as they appear today; the earth has not always looked just like it does right now. According to the

---

* The earth as a whole still acts like a liquid, but its thin outer crust is sufficiently solid to form mountains, as it eventually did.

well-established theory of plate tectonics, the continents ride on various plates of rock which make up the earth's surface. The center of the earth is a very active environment, and it constantly pushes these plates around. Where these plates collide, "subduction" areas form where matter is drawn back down into the earth's molten center; where they separate, volcanic activity fills in the opening cracks. The continents ride around on these moving masses, sometimes splitting apart or crashing into each other. This motion is a little bit like how foam might float around on the surface of a boiling pot of water.

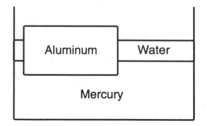

Although aluminum will not float in water, it will float in mercury. It will float high enough to break through a layer of water. The continents do not float on the oceans but they do float on heavier rocks.

Geologists tell us that as recently as a couple of hundred million years ago, all of the continents were briefly unified into a single land mass which they refer to as "Pangea."[31] This clumping together is believed to have happened at other earlier times during the earth's past as well. At the time the dry land first appeared, the waters might literally have been gathered into "one place." But the fact that the Bible also refers to the waters as "seas" (plural—as opposed to the singular implied by the phrase "one place") seems to indicate that the actual physical arrangement, over time, may have been somewhat more complicated.

God also describes the creation and gathering of the seas in Job:

> Who shut up the sea behind doors when it burst forth
> from the womb, when I made the clouds its garment
> and wrapped it in thick darkness, when I fixed limits
> for it and set its doors and bars in place, when I said,
> "This far you may come and no farther . . ."
>
> —Job 38:8-11

It is likely that there would have been at least as much water in the clouds during this early part of the third "day" as there is during any present-day rainstorm; those clouds would have been very dark—hence God's phrase "wrapped it in thick darkness." Of course the "doors" are figurative (see Job 3:10; Psalm 78:23); they refer to the limits which were imposed on the sea as it was gathered and the dry land appeared.

According to the scientific account, the figurative "womb" from which the primordial sea originally "burst" was the earth's rocks. God's words "burst forth" appear to be quite descriptive of the volcanic eruptions and hydrothermal activity which eventually released this water. As explained, this steam then condensed upon the earth's surface to cover it completely with a single giant ocean (when the waters below were divided from those above). Here limits are being set for this ocean as the continents appear.

Again, we see a remarkable agreement between the old-earth interpretation of the biblical account and the scientific account of the earth's beginnings. The Bible is not telling us fairy tales; in this case, it appears that the scientists aren't either. Both witnesses seem to have their accounts grounded upon actual truth.

Genesis 1:11-13

> Then God said, "Let the land produce vegetation:
> seed-bearing plants and trees on the land that bear
> fruit with seed in it, according to their various kinds."
> And it was so. The land produced vegetation: plants
> bearing seed according to their kinds and trees
> bearing fruit with seed in it according to their kinds.

> And God saw that it was good. And there was evening,
> and there was morning—the third day.

As we examine the various created life forms, we will need
to make an adjustment to our traditional view of Genesis. If
the "days" of creation were of indefinite length (as has been
determined), it seems reasonable that they might have had
indefinite edges as well. A particular act of creation, which
had been initiated on a particular "day," might continue into
and overlap subsequent "days." Thus Genesis might reflect
topical as well as chronological organization to some extent;
the creation of all plant types could be reported under one
heading whether or not every single plant "kind" was created
during that same distinct time slot.

There are quite a number of instances where the scientific
information demands overlapping creative "days." According
to the fossil evidence, there are a great many types of plants
(described under day three) which God did not create until
after He had created some types of fish (day five). For
example, the first sharks were created during the Devonian
period (about 400 million years ago);[32] but the first flowering
plants were not created until more recently (200 million years
ago or less).[33] This should not be a surprise; building up a
functioning planetary ecosystem is a tricky business and
requires that new species be introduced in a carefully planned
order. Flowering plants, for example, require certain insects
to pollinate them; God would naturally have held off creating
them until His creation was ready for them. We must conclude that at least some of the creative "days" had overlapping
edges.

Here we will compare the order in which Genesis presents
each of life's forms with the order in which scientists say the
first representatives of each category appeared. This will not
be a trivial task for several reasons. First, God did not necessarily group His creatures into the same categories that scientists or even theologians use. Next, scientists get their
information from fossils, which are hardly ever as plentiful as

one would like. Also, it is not known if *first* appearance is even what Genesis addresses; it might address when the *majority* of a category's types were created. These are just a few of the problems which will be encountered.

Of the many living things God created, the first ones the Bible tells us about appear to be land plants (Genesis 1:11-13). It is tempting to interpret this to mean that the first life was *not* created in the water, as the scientists tell us, but on the land instead. Such a claim is made in *Scientific Creationism*.[34] It would be more accurate, however, to say that the first created life forms the Bible *mentions* are those plants God created upon the land. The Bible does not tell us whether God had created other plants in the water before this time. The fossil evidence tells us that He had created blue-green algae (a single-celled, plantlike life form) in the earth's oceans even before He created the continents.

In this very concise one-chapter account, God has not told us everything He did! A great deal must have happened of which we have not been told anything. In Genesis 1, God mentions the creation of land plants, aquatic animals, birds, and land animals. There are animals which do not fit into any of these categories—amphibians, for example.

Amphibians, such as toads, hatch from eggs in the water, as do fish, but they later undergo modification and relocate to live on the land. Hence they are not exactly water or land animals. Although toads are not specifically mentioned here, or anywhere else in the Bible, they are certainly among God's creatures.

The Bible does not provide a single clue as to when God might have created amphibians. (Yes, I know about the Egyptian plague of frogs in Exodus 8:1-6, but I'm looking for something a little more primordial here.) For all we know from Scripture, amphibians could have been created before plants were. If scientists are understanding God's creation correctly, then they have provided the missing information;

God created the first amphibians between the time He created the first fish and when He created the first true birds.*

Blue-green algae, the oldest known water-living plantlike life form, is not among those categories which God has named in Genesis 1. In fact, God makes no mention of any aquatic plants in that chapter. Therefore we have no scriptural authority for telling the scientists that life did not first appear in the water. All we have a right to say, *if* we are interpreting the Bible correctly, is that the first terrestrial (landliving) plants were created before the first aquatic animals were.

Even this will cause some trouble; scientific sources often have this detail the other way around. The oldest known aquatic animals appear about 500-600 million years ago, during an "explosive" episode of creation at the beginning of the Cambrian period. By comparison, the oldest known terrestrial plants do not appear in the fossil record until about 400 million years ago. Although scientists do not know of any terrestrial plants which preceded aquatic animals, such plants may have existed anyhow.

A lack of fossil evidence does not prove that a particular life form did not exist. In the first place, plants do not often have hard parts and therefore do not fossilize well.** This causes the fossil evidence to be misleading.[35] Next, fossils are much more likely to form on sea floors where sediments are piling up than on the dry land where soil is more likely to get washed away.[36] This makes any terrestrial fossils rare. Furthermore, scientists regard the fossil record in general as being very sketchy from this far back in time.[37]

---

* Amphibians did crawl out of the primordial waters then, just as they still crawl from ponds today. They are cited in biology textbooks as an "evolutionary link" between fish and reptiles as if fish, by their own pioneering spirit, were able to take over the continents. God did create animals (like frogs) which can leave the water to live on the land, but it does not follow from this that naturalistic evolution is true.

** They have no bones or shells; however, seeds fossilize better than most plant parts do.

If some terrestrial plants did precede the first aquatic animals, it is not at all clear that they should have left evidence in the fossil record. Scientists know from geological evidence that the bulk of the continental crust had formed by 2.5 billion years ago;[38] but what may or may not have been living on that dry land has not yet been seen in the fossil record preceding about 400 million years ago.

Because of this lack of actual evidence, there is some disagreement between sources as to what was happening on the dry land while the first aquatic animals were appearing. One source describes the land as "a barren, lifeless desert."[39] Another source says, "The initial 'greening' of the landscape by green algae and bacteria may have taken place at or before this time." (Here "this time" appears to refer to when oxygen first became abundant—long before the first aquatic animals.)[40] As was explained in chapter 5, we should be skeptical in those cases where witnesses disagree; contradicting testimony cannot be adequately founded upon truth. The opinions of the scientists will, therefore, have to be disregarded until they have found evidence on which to ground their claims. As soon as real evidence becomes available, the scientists will present a more unified witness.

About two billion years ago (after the continents had formed but before the first evidence of multicelled aquatic animals) there was a significant change in the composition of the earth's atmosphere. Evidence from iron oxide in mineral deposits indicates that this was when the atmosphere first began containing large amounts of oxygen.[41] Scientists tell us this was because the earth's aquatic blue-green algae had finally started making headway against the processes which were removing oxygen from the atmosphere.

Because God created blue-green algae about three and a half billion years ago, it had already been living in the earth's seas for more than a billion years by this time. If the algae had made no headway in a billion years, it seems unlikely that it would ever produce any spectacular results on its own. It seems more likely that God had created some other plant types by this time which were now assisting in the production of oxygen.

When oxygen is present, an ozone layer begins to form in the upper atmosphere. This ozone layer protects land plants from the sun's harmful ultraviolet radiation. Any land plants which God created before this time would have needed to be very tough or else they would have needed to be physically sheltered.[42] With time, oxygen levels and the subsequent thickness of the ozone layer increased. By about one billion years ago, the atmospheric oxygen had increased to about 4 percent of its present value.[43] With this added margin of protection, God might have created a slightly wider variety of plant types. This in turn would have built up the ozone layer faster, allowing a yet greater variety of plants and so on. The scientific evidence tells us that, starting two billion years ago, the oxygen level began climbing at a faster and faster rate until just under half a billion years ago when it reached nearly its present value.[44]

Although this may be a reasonable description of God's timing as He introduced new land plant types, we don't really know when God might have introduced what type. Because of the lack of fossils, we have very little scientific evidence with which to test our theories.

There is also the question of whether the Bible really restricts this event to *land* plants only. The Hebrew word translated "land" here in verses 11 and 12 is "erets," which can mean the dry land as opposed to the seas (as it does in verse 10), but it can also refer to the whole planet, oceans included, as opposed to the heavens.[45] Either way, whether terrestrial or aquatic, the Bible appears to require that some significantly new plant forms must have been created at about this time. Atmospheric oxygen levels seem to confirm at least this much.

Although this question is not settled either biblically or scientifically, I strongly suspect that the first land plants were created much earlier than the earliest ones known to science.

Scientists are unjustified in claiming the absence of Precambrian terrestrial plant life on such poor authority as the absence of evidence which probably would not have survived in any case. It is possible that this evidence might still be discovered at some time in the future. Perhaps more digging (literally) on the part of the scientists will turn up some actual terrestrial fossils from the time period in question. Meanwhile we must not be dogmatic; we must just be patient and wait.

Another interesting point is that the Bible says that seed-bearing plants and trees (as well as all animals) were created "according to their kinds" (Genesis 1:11,12,21,24).* Traditionally this is understood to mean they will also "reproduce" according to their kinds.[46] The word "reproduce" is not actually part of the biblical statement, but it is so frequently added to it that we may have come to regard it as part of God's Word.

Whether or not the phrase "according to their kinds" means what is usually claimed, it is still true that God created each of the various "kinds" of animals; they did not create themselves. This runs contrary to the spirit of Darwin's theory of gradual and continuous evolution, but the fossil record has stubbornly borne out Genesis and not Darwin in this regard. New "kinds" of life seem to appear, as if from nowhere, and then remain essentially unchanged for their entire stay on the planet—in many cases, for a great many millions of years![47] Here the traditional understanding of the Bible has stood firmly where the most popular scientific *theory* has needed continuous readjustment.

---

* The exact meaning of "kind" (Hebrew "miyn") is not clearly distinguished by ancient Hebrew. The word could mean form, species, kind, or sort. Gesenius' Hebrew-Chaldee Lexicon to the Old Testament, © 1979, Baker Book House, MI, p. 470, entry #4327. The biologists have not been much help either as their definitions are not very firm — and are usually based on evolutionary assumptions. I have some very specific opinions about this and may explain them in another book.

DAY 4
THE GREAT LIGHTS

Genesis 1:14-19

And God said, "Let there be lights in the expanse of the sky to separate the day from the night, and let them serve as signs to mark seasons and days and years, and let them be lights in the expanse of the sky to give light on the earth." And it was so. God made two great lights—the greater light to govern the day and the lesser light to govern the night. He also made the stars. God set them in the expanse of the sky to give light on the earth, to govern the day and the night, and to separate light from darkness. And God saw that it was good. And there was evening, and there was morning—the fourth day.

This presents another apparent difficulty; according to the traditional interpretation of this passage, the sun is being "made" a second time. The scientists assure us that the sun was burning brightly long before there were any plants upon the earth; the Bible tells us that light preceded vegetation. We must agree with both. Plants *do* need light to grow. Furthermore, because light can be seen from very distant stars—light which has been in transit for as long as our sun has been around—we know there must have been plenty of stars back then too.

Scientists are just beginning to agree on how the moon was formed. The leading theory—the one best explaining the evidence collected by the Apollo flights—is that the moon formed from debris which was knocked into orbit when a roughly Mars-sized chunk of matter collided with the earth early on during the formation of the solar system. The evidence places the time of the moon's formation within the latter stages of the earth's formation—about 4.5 billion years ago.[48]

Another minor complication is that it appears that God is telling us that He "set" the sun, moon, and stars in the "expanse" (the space between the waters) rather than in outer space where they certainly are. But of course the word that meant the "expanse" between the waters could also refer to the "expanse" of outer space. Words do have multiple meanings.

Because of these complications, it seems we need to have either another understanding of verses 14-19, or another understanding of Genesis 1:3 and of all the scientific evidence as well. Something did happen at about this time which may provide an explanation.

During the second day, the waters were divided into liquid water below and very thick dark clouds above. At that time, a hypothetical observer standing on the surface of the earth (perhaps in a boat) would have no way of knowing that there were stars or even a sun; the clouds would have been too thick. He would know about day and night but would have no way of knowing that the brighter sky of the day was illuminated from behind by the sun. He would not be able to observe how the sun's arc across the sky would be higher in the summer than in the winter. He would not be able to observe the summer stars as they replaced the winter ones and then were, in turn, replaced themselves. In other words, he would not have the sun, moon and stars to tell him of the days, seasons, and years. He would have the continuing cycle of light and darkness,[49] but that would be all.

By the fourth day, the earth's atmosphere was going through some changes (probably under the influence of the newly created plant types). It appears that this is when (and possibly how) God caused the cloud cover to thin and finally to break up. At this point, it would seem to our earthbound observer (who by now has some land to stand on) that the sun and stars had just come into being. Furthermore they would appear to him to be in the sky rather than in outer space—of which he knows nothing. To him, it would appear as if they had not existed at all until that moment. From that time on, but not before, they would be visible for him to use for reckoning days, seasons, and years. This would put these verses in the class called "observer true"—like those verses which say "the sun rose," when in fact the sun stayed where it was as the earth turned toward it.

This explanation of these verses—that they apply to the first presentation of the formerly hidden sun, moon, and stars—is compatible with the Hebrew words God used. There are only two words from which the difficulty actually arises, "made" used in "God *made* two great lights" and "set" used in "God *set* them in the expanse of the sky." "Made" is translated from the Hebrew "asah" and "set" from the Hebrew "nathan." Where our English translations say "he also made the stars," the Hebrew merely says "also the stars."[50] Other than the way these words have been translated, there is no problem with this passage referring to the breaking up of the clouds.* These words will be examined here.[51]

"Asah," the Hebrew word for "made," is a different word than the one used in the first verse where God "created" the heavens and the earth. There the word was "bara" which can mean "to cut or carve out," "to create or produce," "to begat," or "to feed or grow fat."[52] The word "asah" has a slightly different shade of meaning; it means "to labor," "to work about (or upon) anything," "to make," or "to produce by labor."[53] "Asah" is translated many different ways. Some biblical examples (in the KJV) are: to *deal* kindly (Genesis 24:49), to *work* in gold (Exodus 31:4), to *commit* a sin (Leviticus 5:17), to *prepare* bread (Genesis 27:17), or even to *show* kindness (Genesis 24:12).[54]

The KJV translated "asah" as "do" more than it translated it any other way, more than twice as many times as it translated

---

* Some creationists would disagree with this based on their theories concerning Noah's flood. Of course theological theories are not the same thing as scriptural truth. Here we need only concern ourselves that we are in agreement with the Bible's actual words.

it "make"—which was the second most common rendering. Still the most precise* translation would be more like to "prepare" or "produce." These carry more of the actual color of "asah" than does the nondescript "do." It would be more accurate to say that a cow *produces* milk than that a cow *does* milk ("asah" is translated "gives" milk in Isaiah 7:22).

The most exact translation might go something like, "And God *produced* two great lights."[55] This tells us nothing about how they got there. The translation that God *made* two great lights actually adds a shade of meaning (something like "built") which the Hebrew doesn't necessarily carry. Another translator could just as properly have added a different shade of meaning such as "worked on"; this would be as close to "asah" as "make" is. "Bring forth" is even an acceptable translation for the word (Leviticus 25:21 KJV). It would seem that "asah" is a versatile enough word that it would fit properly almost regardless of how God caused the sun, moon, and stars to appear in the sky.

The Hebrew word "nathan" is also translated in a wealth of different ways. Biblical examples (KJV) include to *deliver* someone (Genesis 32:16), to *bring* a snare (Proverbs 29:25) to *put* out a hand (Genesis 38:28), or to *make* a covenant (Genesis 17:2). The most common translation of "nathan" is "give."[56] The KJV translated "nathan" as "give" more than five times as often as it translated it any other way.

Instead of "God *set* them in the expanse of the sky," the Hebrew merely says, "God *gave* them in the expanse . . ." "Set" carries the idea of a relocation—a meaning which is not necessarily implied by "nathan." Here it would improve the English grammar without altering the Hebrew meaning to use a synonym of "gave" and say that God "presented" them (as in Ezekiel 20:28 KJV). "Nathan," like "asah," will fit with almost

---

*Here the term "most precise" is used instead of the translator's technical term "most literal" to avoid confusion with the other sense of the term "literal" (as opposed to spiritual, figurative, or symbolic). By the term "most literal" a translator merely means the most exact or most common translation.

any theory we might propose. Again it seems we have a rather versatile word.

This verse can be translated so the sky assumes the sense of a display window through which the presentation is made rather than the location where the great lights would be placed; this interpretation removes any problem of apparent misplacement. If the Bible had been translated to allow for modern scientific information, Genesis 1:14-18 might read:

> And God said, "Let there be lights in the expanse of the sky to separate between day and night. Let them be as signs for seasons, and days, and years. And let them be for lights in the expanse of the sky to give light to the earth." And it was so. And God produced two great lights—the greater light to rule the day and the lesser to rule the night, also the stars. God presented them in the expanse of the sky to light the earth and to govern over the day and the night and to separate between light and darkness. And God saw that it was good.[57]

This is actually closer to the original Hebrew than most English translations are. A slightly more scientifically biased rendering, although as accurate as other English translations, could have replaced "produced" with "brought forth." This would be more consistent with previously created astronomical objects being revealed by the removal of a thick cloud cover.

Notice also that the order of appearance is consistent with the idea that these lights became increasingly visible through a decreasing cloud cover. The order of appearance begins with those which are the most easily seen through the clouds and proceeds to those which are least easily seen. First the sun, next the moon, and finally the stars would become visible.

Of course, God's use of such versatile words as "asah" and "nathan" does not prove that He did not actually construct the sun, moon, and stars right then; those words could be taken either way. But they do allow harmony between the fourth-day description and what is known to be the truth from other evidence. The Bible says there was light back in verse three; there is good scientific evidence that this light came from the sun. Because we are not changing the meaning of any of the original Hebrew words, interpreting them in a non-traditional manner is justified. When the scientific data is also considered, we have more total information than most translators do.

DAY 5
FISH AND BIRDS

Genesis 1:20-23

And God said, "Let the water teem with living creatures, and let birds fly above the earth across the
expanse of the sky." So God created the great creatures of the sea and every living and moving thing
with which the water teems, according to their
kinds, and every winged bird according to its kind.
And God saw that it was good. God blessed them
and said, "Be fruitful and increase in number and
fill the water in the seas, and let the birds increase
on the earth." And there was evening, and there
was morning—the fifth day.

Here, the Bible says God created aquatic creatures and
birds—probably in the order mentioned. The scientists are a
little more specific: The first known multicelled aquatic
animal life appeared 500 or 600 million years ago. True fishes
first appeared a little later—about 400 million years ago.

There were some particular episodes during earth's history when many species appeared within what geologists call a
mere "instant." (The rest of us would say many millions of
years.) The creation of aquatic animals was probably the most
remarkable of these episodes. Scientists call this event the
"Cambrian explosion." The term "explosion" was appropri-
ately selected because of the appearance of almost every imag-
inable form of aquatic life within a very short period of time.[58]
The only category of animals which was not represented in this
initial "explosion" was the chordate group (animals with spinal
cords), and even these appeared later during the Cambrian
period. This is an interesting companion to the Bible's phrase
"Let the water teem with living creatures." The two almost certainly refer to the same event. Notice this match confirms the
very nature of this appearance as well as the mere fact of it.
Here is another impressive match between the old-earth understanding of Genesis and the scientific evidence.

True feathered birds—although having teeth—first appeared with the dinosaurs about 150 million years ago. This date is perhaps a little shaky. In order to fly, birds must have lightweight bones. Hence they do not fossilize very well. (Birds fossilize better than plants do, however.) The oldest birds known to scientists might not truly be the very oldest ones.

Interestingly, the word "bird" may also have caused some confusion. "Bird" is translated from the Hebrew "owph" which means merely "a wing."[59] It also carries the idea of "wing covered."[60] This is not necessarily a bird. In Leviticus, for example, this word is used in conjunction with a grasshopper! "There are, however, some **winged** creatures that walk on all fours that you may eat" (Leviticus 11:21, emphasis added). The emphasized word in this verse was translated from the Hebrew "owph."

Even though grasshoppers are not "birds" as we understand the term, they are still included in the biblical category of "owph." In this same chapter of Leviticus, "owph" is also used in reference to a bat (compare verses 13 and 19). We must keep reminding ourselves that Genesis, like Leviticus, was written a long time ago; we should not be surprised if we have to temporarily lay aside our modern understanding of animal classifications if we are to interpret it correctly. Genesis was written in ancient Hebrew, not in modern technical English.

It would seem that God may include flying insects in with His category of "owph." (He may even have included *all* "bugs.")* This pushes the date for the first appearance of "owph" back to about 350 million years ago[61]—to about the time of the first amphibians. This is farther back than any other exclusively land-dwelling animal including the dinosaurs, but after the first aquatic animals.

---

* Scorpions, for example, appear in the fossil record before winged insects. Although the Bible mentions scorpions many times, it does not specify how they are to be classified.

DAY 6
LAND ANIMALS AND MEN

Genesis 1:24,25

And God said, "Let the land produce living creatures according to their kinds: livestock, creatures that move along the ground, and wild animals, each according to its kind." And it was so. God made the wild animals according to their kinds, the livestock according to their kinds, and all the creatures that move along the ground according to their kinds. And God saw that it was good.

These two verses primarily refer to mammals—most of which have appeared only within the last 65 million years. The oldest dinosaurs date from roughly 230 million years ago. Because dinosaurs did "move" along the ground and were "wild animals," it seems reasonable to include them here. That would make this category older than the oldest known true birds. Therefore, if we were to disallow bugs from the bird category, this would cause a chronology problem.

This discrepancy might just reflect an unfortunate lack of bird fossils; as has been explained, the fossil evidence for birds is not as complete as that for the dinosaurs. However, a lack of fossils is probably not the explanation. If God included winged insects—or *all* "bugs"—in with His group "birds," this would completely eliminate the chronology problem (since "bugs" appeared before any other land animals). It is not at all a conventional approach, but it is a possible way to solve the problem without abandoning the scientific or scriptural evidence.

Genesis 1:26,27

Then God said, "Let us make man in our image, in our likeness, and let them rule over the fish of the sea and the birds of the air, over the livestock, over all the

> earth, and over all the creatures that move along the
> ground." So God created man in his own image, . . .

This brings us up to God's last creation: man is the final entry given in Genesis 1. The oldest creature that anyone ever dares to call a man, *Homo habilis,* appeared about two or three million years ago.[62] Even though *Homo habilis* made and used tools (sharp flakes which he chipped off of rocks), he was not really a man.* In fact, he was *quite unlike* modern man.

There are also some more recent manlike creatures: *Homo erectus, Homo sapiens neanderthalensis,* and *Archaic Homo. Homo erectus* first appeared about 1.5 million years ago[63] and *Homo sapiens neanderthalensis* about 150,000 years ago.[64] This last date falls in the dating gap. As explained back in chapter 5, it is difficult to date fossils from this period, so this date should be treated with some caution. *Archaic Homo* is a loosely defined category which is sometimes applied to *Homo erectus* and sometimes to another species of manlike ape which seems to be coming into focus in the fossil record. This new creature is presently thought to fill the gap** between *Homo erectus* and true moderns; this gap was once supposed to have been bridged by the Neanderthals. *Archaic Homo* (the new creature) has sometimes been classified as a Neanderthal[65] and sometimes as a modern.[66] In my opinion, all of these other creatures should be excluded from the category of true men; even though they looked more like men and made more advanced tools than *Homo habilis* did, they still were not men.

The Neanderthals were sufficiently similar to modern men that young-earth creationists usually classify both together as a single group.[67] However, the scientific evidence indicates that modern men could not even interbreed with the Neanderthals.[68] If it is true, as I believe, that God's creatures breed

---

* Some creationists do consider Homo habilis to be a man.

** Even if we are not evolutionists, we need to acknowledge that God's method of creating new species has left behind a "chain" of successive creatures. I have my own theory as to why this should be so, which may be presented in a later book.

true to their "kinds," then we must conclude the Neanderthals were another "kind." They were similar to us, but they were still separate creations of God.

Because God created the different kinds of animals, theologians sometimes insist that there could never have been any manlike ape creatures (denying the scientific evidence). Because God's creation provides evidence that manlike ape creatures existed, scientists sometimes insist that God didn't create the different kinds of animals (denying God's Word). Because I accept both God's Word and the evidence from His creation, I believe that manlike apes existed and were specifically created by God (denying both human theories). The obvious similarities between the manlike apes and modern men do *not* prove we evolved from them, but denying their existence (or ignoring their differences) is a step away from God's truth—not toward it.

Although we may be uncomfortable with the idea of a nonhuman creature who made and used tools, we have no scriptural reason to be. We may wonder *why* God created them,* but we have no scriptural grounds to insist He didn't. Their existence may damage the pride we take in our "lofty" status as humans, but God has never promised us that we had anything to be proud of anyway (Psalm 103:14)—only that we would rule over His creation (Genesis 1:28). We might like to believe we are the only intelligent creatures God ever made, but we are not. The brain design of Neanderthal man was indeed remarkable;[69] and so is that of a modern bottle-nosed dolphin. In fact, a dolphin's brain is larger than a modern man's is. Although a larger brain doesn't prove greater, or even equal, intelligence, dolphins are still very intelligent creatures[70] and God certainly made them. We have to admit we share this planet with other intelligent creatures![71]

---

* I have some definite opinions on this subject which may be presented in a later book. There is some fascinating scriptural evidence which might have led us to expect God's creation of these manlike apes if we had been keeping our eyes open!

Nevertheless, Adam was created in God's image while those other creatures were not. To demonstrate the division between us and them, there is no physical evidence that any of them ever wore clothes—not even for warmth. Although the claim is often made that the Neanderthals wore clothes, there is no supporting evidence—it is merely assumed that they did because they lived in cold climates.[72] There is no physical evidence that they didn't have sufficient body hair for warmth.[73] The first actual evidence of clothing and of bone sewing needles does not appear until fully modern man does.[74] This evidence suggests that the knowledge of sin (and therefore Adam's fall) came with modern man. This is another reason those earlier creatures should not be considered true men.

Many other traits which are normally considered human did not appear until fully modern man either. The earliest undisputed art first appears at the same time as the moderns do.[75] Although scientists recently believed that Neanderthals buried their dead, this idea has now been brought under question.[76] The earliest presently undisputed burials appear at the same time as modern man does. The fossil evidence also indicates that articulate speech was not possible for the Neanderthals. Their vocal tract did not have the right shape.[77]

God made Adam a fully modern man (*Homo sapiens sapiens*). Exactly how long ago modern man appeared is hard to say. History only provides recent dates—from within the last 7,000 years. It is certain that man was around before then, probably *long* before then; it is just difficult to know how much before.

Unfortunately, radioactive-dating techniques are of only limited help here. The event was sufficiently recent that the potassium-argon method has not provided much help, and it is too long ago to be accurately pinpointed by carbon-14. According to sources from a few decades ago, the oldest fossils of modern man date (by carbon-14) to around 35 or 40,000 years ago, but these dates were rather shaky. As explained in chapter 5, carbon-14 needs calibration and at present the calibration has not been worked out this far back.

More recently, some remains promoted as being "fully modern humans" have been found which date (using exotic methods) as early as about 100,000 years old.[78] These fossils are presently classified as "modern men" although some of them are said to display some "primitive features." The supplement (loose poster) to the February 1997 *National Geographic*[79] pictures one of these skulls. That skull is certainly missing the brow ridges of the Neanderthals and of *Archaic Homo*, but the eye and nose sockets look Neanderthal—not human.

Are these fossils truly modern men, as has been claimed? Are they really some new creature which falls between *Archaic Homo* and modern men? Or is something else entirely different going on? Although these questions might keep both scientists and theologians up nights, they really aren't that important to us right here; for the present purposes, it is only important that man fits into his proper place in the chronological order of God's creation. This much has been properly established. The conventional date of 35–40,000 years for the age of *true* men might be correct, but we must allow that it might be substantially in error.

In A.D. 1650, James Ussher,[80] the archbishop of Armagh, attempted to calculate the year in which God created Adam by using the genealogies provided in the Bible. He came up with a date of 4004 B.C.* This is about 6,000 years ago. It does not agree with the scientific evidence which we have just examined. A possible reason for this becomes apparent when we take a closer look at the biblical genealogies.

It can be seen from comparing the genealogies from Genesis with the ones given in Luke[81] that the biblical lists are not as complete as we would like them to be. Luke 3:35,36, for example, records a second Cainan between Arphaxad and

---

* Appendix 5 has been included for anyone who is interested in an attempted reconstruction of Ussher's calculations.

Sala (also spelled Shelah or Salah) which is not found in the parallel genealogy of Genesis 11:12. This is a warning that we can't be certain that Ussher's calculation will give us meaningful dates.

Because of this, even young-earth creationists do not hold rigidly to the 6,000-year age. Most of them assume about 10,000 years ago for the date of the creation of the earth—and therefore of Adam as well. (Remember that they consider Adam to have been created within a mere 144 hours of the time the heavens and earth were created.) For example:

> Furthermore, the genealogies listed in Genesis and elsewhere in the Bible, it is believed, would restrict the time of creation to somewhere between six thousand and about ten thousand years ago.
>
> —*EVOLUTION: THE FOSSILS SAY NO!*[82]

> To the extent that *sound* archaeological research may *require* dating of early human settlements at dates earlier than the traditional Ussher chronology allows, the Bible does indicate the possibility of minor gaps in the genealogies . . .
>
> —*SCIENTIFIC CREATIONISM*[83]

The point here is that even those who hold most rigidly to the traditional interpretation of the biblical text do not regard Ussher's type of computing to be a reliable method of interpreting the Bible. Because there are well-founded historic dates which force human history back farther than these calculations allow,[84] and because of the known existence of some gaps in the genealogies, it might be more reasonable (within some sort of limits) to assume that the historic and archaeological dates are approximately correct.

The authors of *Scientific Creationism* (pp. 247-250) quite reasonably explain that they are reluctant to allow for gaps accounting for the million years which they regard as the evolutionists' measure of human history, but *we are not evolutionists* and are not claiming Adam was a prehuman, manlike ape creature (such as a Neanderthal). We need only account for the age of modern men.

Even so, the age of modern men must constitute a lot of gaps—many tens of thousands of years' worth at the very least. The young-earth creationists seem to be thinking more on the order of merely a few thousand extra years. Dr. Gish, for example, in his book *Evolution: The Fossils Say No!* (quoted above), has allowed for about 4,000 extra years. Because there is no scriptural evidence which limits these gaps to what the young-earth creationists are recommending, it will be assumed here that there are a great many gaps* and that they can account for this discrepancy.

The scientific dating might be somewhat in error, but this won't completely remove the problem. Carbon-14 can be calibrated back farther than the Ussher chronology goes and, at that point, the carbon-14 dates are too young—not too old (see chapter 5). Anyway, there are other kinds of evidence which tend to confirm the carbon-14 dates. Other dating techniques are more suspect, but if we have learned anything at all from this book, we should not just assume they are wrong. It is quite likely that the error lies in *our traditional understanding* of Scripture.

One interesting theory suggests that modern humans have been on the planet for many tens of thousands of years but that the particular, and very special, man named Adam was created within the last 10,000 years. It appears there may be some archaeological evidence which lends support to this theory.[85]

Although we may not be comfortable with either this many gaps or with the possibility of humans who lived before Adam, we have no evidence that the truth should be what we are most comfortable with. Truth can sometimes be hard to hear. Maybe some future advance in the scientific understanding of early man will suddenly throw light on all of the

---

* The Bible sometimes provides extremely abridged genealogies — for example Matthew 1:1, "Jesus Christ, the son of David, the son of Abraham."

presently obscure biblical passages and clear this all up. Perhaps the solution will come through advances in biblical understanding—or even from clay tablets from digs in Iraq. Meanwhile we will have to be patient. It is at times like this that keeping one's eyes open and waiting is the recommended course of action.

Conclusions

The scientific evidence has not been as hard on Genesis 1 as we might have expected. It has been necessary to make a few adjustments to our *traditional understanding*, we had to assume the oldest plant fossils have not yet been discovered, and we still have quite a few unanswered questions, but it has not been necessary to abandon either *scriptural authority* or any actual *scientific evidence*. Cautious interpretation can produce a very remarkable fit—a fit which not only matches the coarse data but some very fine points as well. Instead of opposing the Bible, scientific evidence can elaborate upon it and help us to choose between the different possible interpretations.

God's creation can be used as a powerful commentary on what Genesis really means. Remember, God "wrote" both accounts. What better source is there to consult about what a book means than another book by that very same author—especially one which covers the same information? Of course there is always that author Himself. I would like to encourage you, as you check the Scriptures (and the libraries) to see if this information is correct, to also seek God and ask for His help. His Word would be true even if every man were found to be a liar (Romans 3:4)!

Once again, I want to remind you that none of the ideas presented in this chapter are intended to be dogmatic claims. It is not known for certain which meaning or meanings God actually intended in the Scriptures. The possibilities which have been proposed merely appear to be in harmony with both God's written Word and His created universe as we understand them at the present time. Whether or not this understanding is truth, time will judge. Knowledge will increase and when it does, remaining errors will be exposed. We must continue to test everything, and we must hold on to the good. Furthermore, we must avoid those things which prove to be false (1 Thessalonians 5:21,22).

SUMMARY OF GENESIS CHAPTER ONE

Following is a summary of the statements made in this chapter. The statements are arranged alongside the NIV biblical text to expedite comparison. They are grouped both by scriptural "day" and scientific age.

Day 1
About 15-20 billion years ago

GENESIS 1:1

"In the beginning God created the heavens and the earth."

God created matter, space, and time.

About 4.5 billion years ago

GENESIS 1:2

"Now the earth was formless and empty, darkness was over the surface of the deep, and the Spirit of God was hovering over the waters."

The matter from with God formed our earth and solar system comprised a shapeless nebula in dark space. God set to work on it to accomplish His intentions.

About 4.5 billion years ago

GENESIS 1:3

"And God said, 'Let there be light,' and there was light."

Sunlight became visible from earth at this time. At some point, God caused the sun to ignite, as a giant, continuously burning hydrogen bomb.

This verse may either refer to this ignition or to when God cleared some of the nebular dust away.

GENESIS 1:4,5

"God saw that the light was good, and he separated the light from the darkness. God called the light 'day,' and the darkness he called 'night.' And there was evening, and there was morning—the first day."

God finished clearing the nebular dust away and the earth cooled. The earth's back side became dark. Its original atmosphere was stripped.

Day 2
About 4 billion years ago

GENESIS 1:6-8

"And God said, 'Let there be an expanse between the waters to separate water from water.' So God made the expanse and separated the water under the expanse from the water above it. And it was so. God called the expanse 'sky.' And there was evening, and there was morning—the second day."

The earth cooled some more. Some of the volcanic steam which now surrounded it condensed into water which covered the earth's surface. God made an air space between the dark clouds and the surface water.

Day 3
About 2.5-3 billion years ago

GENESIS 1:9,10

"And God said, 'Let the water under the sky be gathered to one place, and let dry ground appear.' And it was so. God called the dry ground 'land,' and the gathered waters he called 'seas.' And God saw that it was good."

God caused the earth's crust to form continents which pushed up through the oceans. (God had created single-celled plant-like aquatic life by this time.)

Possibly 1-2 billion years ago

GENESIS 1:11-13

"Then God said, 'Let the land produce vegetation: seed-bearing plants and trees on the land that bear fruit with seed in it, according to their various kinds.' And it was so. The land produced vegetation: plants bearing seed according to their kinds and trees bearing fruit with seed in it according to their kinds. And God saw that it was good. And there was evening, and there was morning—the third day."

The first terrestrial plants were probably created at this time. There is, as yet, no fossil evidence for them. Large amounts of oxygen first appeared in the atmosphere about two billion years ago. God continued to create other kinds of plants during subsequent "days."

Day 4
Possibly 1 billion years ago
(a *very* rough guess)

GENESIS 1:14-19

"And God said, 'Let there be lights in the expanse of the sky to separate the day from the night, and let them serve as signs to mark seasons and days and years, and let them be lights in the expanse of the sky to give light on the earth.' And it was so. God made two great lights—the greater light to govern the day and the lesser light to govern the night. He also made the stars. God set them in the expanse of the sky to give light on the earth, to govern the day and the night, and to separate light from darkness. And God saw that it was good. And there was evening, and there was morning—the fourth day."

God "brought forth" the sun, moon, and stars in that order by clearing the thick cloud layer from around the earth. He "presented" them in the heavens where they could be used for the figuring of seasons, days and years.

Day 5
About 500-600 million years ago

GENESIS 1:20-23

"And God said, 'Let the water teem with living creatures, and let birds fly above the earth across the expanse of the sky.' So God created the great creatures of the sea and every living and moving thing with which the water teems, according to their kinds, and every winged bird according to its kind. And God saw that it was good. God blessed them and said, 'Be fruitful and increase in number and fill the water in the seas, and let the birds increase on the earth.' And there was evening, and there was morning—the fifth day."

God created an "explosion" of aquatic life forms at this time. He began making true fish a little later—400 million years ago. The first "winged creatures" were insects, created 350 million years ago. God made the first amphibians 300–350 million years ago. The oldest known true feathered birds appear overlapping day six—during the time of the dinosaurs.

Day 6
About 230 million years ago

Genesis 1:24,25

"And God said, 'Let the land produce living creatures according to their kinds: livestock, creatures that move along the ground, and wild animals, each according to its kind.' And it was so. God made the wild animals according to their kinds, the livestock according to their kinds, and all the creatures that move along the ground according to their kinds. And God saw that it was good."

God made the reptiles, including the dinosaurs, beginning about 230 million years ago. Most mammals were created later—beginning 65 million years ago. God created the first tool-using manlike apes about 2–3 million years ago.

Possibly 40 thousand years ago

Genesis 1:26,27

"Then God said, 'Let us make man in our image, in our likeness, and let them rule over the fish of the sea and the birds of the air, over the livestock, over all the earth, and over all the creatures that move along the ground.' So God created man in his own image. . . . "

God created Adam a fully modern human.

8

Repairing
the Damage

Always be prepared to give an answer to everyone who
asks you to give the reason for the hope that you have.
But do this with gentleness and respect.

— 1 PETER 3:15, EMPHASIS ADDED

As explained at the beginning of this book, we have
been instructed to remove errors from our own arguments
before we attempt to correct atheists (Matthew 7:5). Consequently, the church must abandon the young-earth position. This applies to *all of us*—not just the relatively small
number of vocal creationists who are promoting the young-
earth error in their lectures and books. Leaders without followers are not really leaders at all. Therefore we are all
responsible and must all do what we can to correct the
error.

Probably the most important first step which we need to
take is to avoid laughing when an atheist is made out to be a
fool by a Christian. Participating in ridicule is a way of
showing someone that we have judged him to be a fool. "The
fool says in his heart, 'There is no God.'" (Psalm 14:1). But

we should never laugh—not even at true fools. In Matthew, Jesus warns us:

> Do not judge, or you too will be judged. For in the same way you judge others, you will be judged, and with the measure you use, it will be measured to you.
>
> —MATTHEW 7:1,2

Here Jesus has all but promised us that if we laugh at a fool, we will come to discover that we ourselves have been fools. In fact, the Proverbs seem to lump fools and mockers (or scorners) together as a single group (for example, Proverbs 1:22).

More importantly, we must remember that our goal is to lead atheists to Christ—not to drive them farther away! Every time a scientist has said (correctly) that some particular fossil was millions of years old, and we mocked him, judging him to be a fool, we have actually driven him further from salvation. Now we have come to find that we ourselves have been the fools; we have been rude fools too—laughing openly at men who told us the truth. Consider this too: We have laughed at men who knew they spoke the truth and then watched us laugh. They are not likely to take us very seriously; it is more likely that they will consider us an enemy to the truth—an enemy which must be excluded from any position of public influence.

Perhaps we have a zeal for God but, unfortunately, this zeal is not always according to knowledge (like Romans 10:2). Paul the apostle originally channeled his powerful zeal for God against the early church. What are we doing with ours? The efforts of young-earth creationists have made Christianity look foolish by associating it with a position which is simply false. It would have been much better if those creationists had spent their time suggesting consistent structures of ideas which actually explain the scientific facts.

Zealous young earthers have done something which is worse than just promoting a false position. When erring young-earth arguments were made, how were they supported? Were the scientific facts the only things which were misrepresented? Might the *scientists* also have been misrepresented? Consider this reaction by Harvard's Stephen Gould:

> Faced with these facts of evolution and the philosophical bankruptcy of their own position, creationists rely upon distortion and innuendo to buttress their rhetorical claim. If I sound sharp or bitter, indeed I am—for I have become a major target of these practices.[1]

We have not used good science or good manners—it is well known that we have not. The evolutionists certainly have not been righteous either, but there will be time to address that—*after* we get our own act together.

Much of the teaching of evolution is founded upon "religious" atheism instead of scientific evidence. This is why evolutionists have such religious faith in what they call the "facts of evolution." Because evolution is an inferred generalization, not directly observable data, it cannot possibly be a fact.* It would be nice if we creationists were in a position to point this out to them, but we are not likely to be heard. None of us will be taken seriously. It is assumed that all creationists are careless about their facts. If only we could just start afresh! But we cannot; sin always leaves scars—even when the real price has been paid for us.

We are losing an important battle—not against true science, but against another religion. Evolutionism is being preached in our schools and courtrooms and is beginning to interfere with our personal lives. We live in a society which systematically eliminates biblical teaching of any kind from *our* public schools under the pretense of separation of church and state, yet *our* children are subjected to years of atheistic "religious" indoctrination. Furthermore, this mischief is

---

* I am convinced that naturalistic macroevolution is not even a valid theory, but merely an error.

funded by *our* tax dollars! There is a great deal at stake here; we desperately need to be taken seriously.

This is not likely to happen—especially since the textbooks which young-earth creationists have offered as a substitute contain scientific errors everywhere the subject of dates occurs. If young-earth creationists had not done such a poor job of presenting God's creation, then we probably would not now be hearing atheists tell us that evolution is a "fact." The evolutionists' arguments only look good when they are compared to young-earth arguments; if the latter were not so bad, the former would not look at all plausible. The evolutionary view is not really convincing.

People have not been intellectually forced into atheism by the world's data; God has left enough evidence for His existence. His own account of how He created our universe is pleading for recognition. Naturalistic evolution is a position which men have taken in spite of a great deal of data. Some have taken this position to avoid having to give an account to their Creator. Others might feel we creationists have left them no viable alternative.

We may wonder how they could be so foolish, but the answer is not really so very far out of reach. Perhaps the evolutionists' "religion" has dulled their brains, but we Christians *also* seem to have forgotten how to think. The difference between 10,000 years and 4.5 billion years is as great as the difference between one inch and seven miles. This is essentially the difference between a fairy tale and real life. We seem to have taught ourselves to think in ways which permit us to look at seven miles and convince ourselves we are seeing one inch. Furthermore, we have taught ourselves to read the Bible in such a way that it seems not only to allow for our error, but to certify it with full scriptural authority. We are *all* humans; and humans are fully capable of being *this wrong!*

There might still be hope, but we must stop insisting that the Bible tells a "fairy tale" about a 10,000-year-old universe. Instead, we must reason out what the truth really is; then our preaching of Christianity could fit the universe's facts as well as the Bible's. Maybe then scientifically educated people would not close their eyes and ears to the truth. As Paul says:

> Since the creation of the world God's invisible quali-
> ties—his eternal power and divine nature—have been
> clearly seen, being understood from what has been
> made, so that **men are without excuse**.
>
> —ROMANS 1:20, EMPHASIS ADDED

If we creationists would simply allow God's universe to speak for us instead of against us, then maybe a few more people would be able to see the hand of God at work in His creation and would come to know the saving truth.

> God so loved the world that he gave his one and only
> Son, that whoever believes in him shall not perish but
> have eternal life. For God did not send his Son into
> the world to condemn the world, but to save the world
> through him.
>
> —JESUS IN JOHN 3:16,17

APPENDIX 1

Predictions

Here I would like to make some predictions based on my understanding of how science and Genesis dovetail—the understanding which has been presented in this book. Those who are interested can test the claims made here with new scientific discoveries as they become available. This will provide a means to help determine if my understanding is correct or if we must look for another one.

1) Precambrian land plants (older than the oldest aquatic animals) should be discovered eventually (assuming the traditional understanding of "erets" as "dry land" is correct).

2) No evidence will ever turn up that men preceding modern man ever wore clothes. (There was no knowledge of sin.) Although it can be argued that clothes were needed for warmth in the Ice Age climate (even if not for modesty), I am betting (perhaps unnecessarily) that the Neanderthals and other prehumans had sufficient body hair.

3) More evidence will continue to sharpen the separation between the Neanderthals and modern men. *Archaic Homo* will eventually resolve into another distinct "kind." Evidence will eventually sharpen

the difference between modern men and the Archaics as well.

4) Something will eventually turn up which will make sense out of the difference between the Ussher chronology (6,000 years or 7,500 years if the Septuagint genealogies are correct—see appendix 5) and the carbon-14 chronology (about 40,000 years).

5) All future young-earth "proofs" will have errors in them. As Christians become educated concerning the simpler errors, young-earth "proofs" will become increasingly complicated so that the errors will be increasingly harder to locate.

APPENDIX 2

Arguments for 24-Hour Days

The following four quotations present arguments in support of the six-consecutive-24-hour interpretation of the days of creation. These sources are quoted here in length to ensure that the arguments are in context.

Source #1:

> Many Christians suggest that we should give God sufficient time to create this complex world by stretching the days of creation into hundreds of millions of years, so that each day of creation would equal an age. Is this legitimate? Well, actually it is amazing, when we begin to study the first chapter of Genesis, to discover that we have a built-in scheme of interpreting the length of these days, which shows that these must have been the same kind of days that we know today. For example, Genesis 1:14 says that God created the lights to divide the day from the night, and that they were to be for signs, for seasons, for days and years. If the days are ages, then what are years? If a day is an age, then what is a night? In other words, the whole passage becomes ridiculous when we begin to stretch or reinterpret the word "day."
>
> It is perfectly correct that in the Bible occasionally the word "day" means a long, indefinite period of time, such as the "Day of the Lord." But never when the word "day" is connected with a number does it mean anything other than a

twenty-four hour period—for instance, the second day, the fourth day, the sixth day. Furthermore, whenever the word "day" is connected with the qualifying phrase "evening and morning," we find a technical Hebrew expression that speaks of the rotation of the Earth's axis in reference to a fixed light source, passing through a night-day cycle.*

Genesis chapter one is explained by Exodus 20:9,11, when God spoke to Israel and said, "Six days shalt thou labour, and do all thy work . . . For in six days the LORD made heaven and earth, the sea, and all that in them is." Obviously God was speaking in terms of literal days. No Jew in his right mind would think that God meant "six indefinite periods shalt thou labor and rest a seventh indefinite period.". . .

(*And God Created*, ed. Kelly L. Segraves, © 1973, Creation-Science Research Center, San Diego, CA, vol. 2, pp. 62,63.)

Source #2:

As has been mentioned before, the Bible does not state the age of the world; consequently, several opinions are held by creationists. They can be divided easily into two major groupings: those who believe that the account of the creation of the world refers to six literal days, and those who feel that the six days were a figurative way of referring to indefinite periods of time. Both have some very good reasons for holding the positions they hold.

Arguments for six literal days are:

1. This would seem to be the normal way to interpret the passage (Gen. 1).

2. The term "day" when used elsewhere in Scripture usually means literal twenty-four hour days.

---

* Author's note: Historically, the understanding that the earth turns on its axis was not even suggested until Aristarchus (born 310 B.C.) nor was the theory made well known until Nicolaus Copernicus A.D. 1473-1543. The Sleepwalkers, Arthur Koestler, © 1959, The Universal Library, Grosset and Dunlap, New York, p. 49. It follows that this idea has no bearing whatsoever on the biblical expression "evening and morning."

3. It is hard to understand the reasoning of the argument of a Sabbath of rest on the seventh day after the six days of work creating the world if they were not six literal days (Gen. 2:2).

(*Creation vs. Evolution Handbook*, Thomas F. Heinze, © 1973, Baker Book House, Grand Rapids, MI, pp. 104-105.)

Source #3:

. . . Many sincere and competent Biblical scholars have felt it so mandatory to accept the geological age system that they have prematurely settled on the so-called day-age theory as the recommended interpretation of Genesis 1. By this device, they seek more or less to equate the days of creation with the ages of evolutionary geology.

However, this theory, no less than the gap theory, encounters numerous overwhelming objections which render it invalid. In the first place, the order of creative events narrated in Genesis 1 is very different from the accepted order of fossils in the rocks representing the geological ages. A number of these contradictions will be noted in the course of the exposition.

Second, as already pointed out when discussing the gap theory, the geological ages are predicated on the fossil record, and fossils speak unequivocally of the reign of suffering and death in the world. The day-age theory, therefore, accepts as real the existence of death before sin, in direct contradiction to the Biblical teaching that death is a divine judgment on man's dominion because of man's sin (Romans 5:12). Thus it assumes that suffering and death comprise an integral part of God's work of creating and preparing the world for man; and this in effect pictures God as a sadistic ogre, not as the Biblical God of grace and love.

Finally, the Biblical record itself makes it plain that the days of creation are literal days, not long indefinite ages. This will become conclusively evident as we examine the actual wording of these verses. Even though it may occasionally be possible for the Hebrew word for "day" (*yom*) to mean an indefinite time, the specific context in Genesis 1 precludes any such meaning here.

If the reader asks himself this question: "Suppose the writer of Genesis wished to teach his readers that all things were created and made in six literal days, then what words would he use to best convey this thought?" he would have to answer that the writer would have used the actual words in Genesis 1. If he wished to convey the idea of long geological ages, however, he could surely have done it far more clearly and effectively in other words than in those which he selected. It was clearly his intent to teach creation in six literal days.

Therefore, the only proper way to interpret Genesis 1 is not to "interpret" it at all. That is, we accept the fact that it was meant to say exactly what it says. The "days" are literal days and the events described happened in just the way described. This incomparable first chapter of Scripture tells us what we could never learn any other way—the history of creation. "For in six days the LORD made heaven and earth, the sea, and all that in them is, and rested the seventh day: wherefore the Lord blessed the sabbath day, and hallowed it" (Exodus 20:11).

. . . The terms "evening" (Hebrew *ereb*) and "morning" (Hebrew *boqer*) each occur more than one hundred times in the Old Testament, and always have the literal meaning— that is, the termination of the daily period of light and the termination of the daily period of darkness, respectively. Similarly, the occurrence of "day" modified by a numeral (e.g., "third day") is a construction occurring more than a hundred times in the Pentateuch alone, always with the literal meaning. Even though it may challenge our minds to visualize the lands and seas, and all plants, being formed in one literal day, that is exactly what the Bible says! We are not justified at all either in questioning God's power to do this or His veracity in telling us that He did.*

(*The Genesis Record*, Henry M. Morris, © 1976, Baker Book House, Grand Rapids, MI, pp. 53,54,64.)

---

* Author's note: Nor are we justified in questioning God's right to create gradually if he so chooses or His veracity in telling us that the scientific evidence speaks the truth (Psalm 19:1,2; Romans 1:20), but we obviously do need to question human theories about God's Word and His creation.

Source #4

Christ says there have been people on the earth since the very beginning of the world—and He ought to know, for He was there!

For example, when the Pharisees asked Him about marriage and divorce, He replied that "from the beginning of the creation God made them male and female" (Mark 10:6). He did *not* say that God made the first man and woman fifteen *billion years after* the beginning of the creation, but right *from* the beginning of the creation.

("Christ and the Time of Creation," Henry M. Morris, Ph.D., Back to Genesis, no. 70, page "a", *Acts & Facts*, October 1994, vol. 23, no. 10, Institute for Creation Research, El Cajon, CA 92021.)

APPENDIX 3

Real World Clocks

A Discussion for Those
Having a Technical Background

This appendix will try to explain the problem of synchronization of clocks in the same way in which it is often presented to beginning physics students. This illustration is silly enough to be interesting, but it is also serious enough to accurately demonstrate the principles involved.

First we must picture in our minds a barn located anywhere in space (or on a planet) with two doors which open outward on the two opposite front and back walls. We will assume that those two doors are 9 meters apart. Next we will picture a pole vaulter who is traveling very fast and carrying a 10-meter pole. If the two doors are both open, the pole vaulter can run (carrying his pole) in through the front door, through the barn, and out through the back door without any difficulty. There will, of course, be a short period of time when his pole will extend out of the barn through both doors at the same time.

Next we will make our pole vaulter run very fast—80 percent of the speed of light—and have him run through the barn again. This time the effects of Einstein's special theory of relativity will be apparent. If we stand next to the barn and observe the pole vaulter, his pole will appear to us (in our stationary frame of reference) to have shortened to a new length equal to its original length (10 meters) times the square root of $(1-v^2/c^2)$.[1] Because our vaulter is running at 80 percent light speed, v/c is 0.8 and so v^2/c^2 will become 0.64, which when subtracted from 1 leaves 0.36, whose square root is 0.6. When we multiply this factor by the original length of the pole (10 meters), we find that the pole now appears to us (in our frame of reference) to be only 6 meters long.

So at this speed, the pole fits easily into the 9 meter barn. This means there is a very brief instant, while the vaulter is running through the barn, when we could very quickly slam both doors *at the same time* and open them again before there was any problem. We could, in principle at least, take a picture of the entire pole safely inside the barn with both doors closed. So far there is no problem.

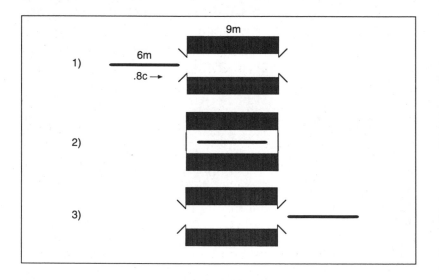

Now, how does this appear in the pole vaulter's frame of reference? It is a basic precept of relativity that all experiments must give the same results when viewed from any frame of reference. According to *Modern Physics:*

As the Michelson-Morley experiment revealed, there is *no* ether,* and therefore no way of specifying any universal frame of reference. In other words, if we observe something changing its position with respect to us, we have no way (even in principle) of knowing whether *it* is moving or *we* are moving.[2]

So now we must look at this from the pole vaulter's frame of reference. Let us assume that it is the pole vaulter who is standing still (we ourselves will be standing beside him) and that it is the barn which is whizzing by around us at 80 percent light speed. This time it is the barn that appears to shorten by the same 0.6 factor (because the relative velocity, v/c, is still 0.8)—to a length of 9 meters times 0.6 which is equal to 5.4 meters. The 10-meter pole will no longer fit!

So what is going to happen when both of the barn's doors are closed *at the same time* as they were when we observed the way the universe behaves as seen from the barn's frame of reference? When the pole vaulter finally sits down after the experiment has been completed to discuss its results with the observer who stood by the barn, will they disagree as to whether or not there was a collision? Will the pole vaulter show his splintered pole as evidence and the barn observer show a motion-picture sequence which proves that the pole was never even touched? Of course not! There cannot be any evidence, even in principle, which would prove in any absolute sense whether it was "they" or "we" who were moving.

As we saw in chapter 4, the phrase *at the same time* is completely without meaning when high speeds or large distances are involved. If this phrase had any meaning, then we would have an unresolvable paradox here, but the phrase has no meaning and, as we will see, we do not have a paradox.

---

* Author's note: The term "ether" refers to a hypothetical "fluid" that light waves were once thought to travel through. It was supposed to be the absolute universal stationary frame of reference.

Let us return to our example. We will have an observer, who is standing by the barn, decide when to close and reopen the two doors. (We will give him very long arms so that he can close and reopen both doors *at the same time*.)

What would happen, according to Einstein's laws, is that the pole vaulter would see this single event (both doors closing and reopening) as two separate events. First he would see the barn's back door (the one he would pass through last) close and reopen while the leading end of his pole (although well inside the barn) was still a safe distance from that door. (2a). This would be before the hind end of the pole had made it into the barn at all.

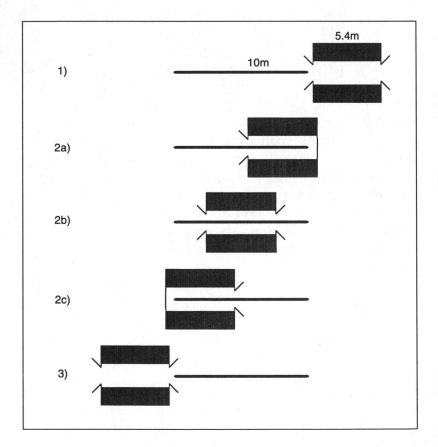

An instant later (*not at the same time*), he would see the front door (the one he passed through first) close and reopen, but only after the hind end of the pole was safely inside the barn and clear of that door (2c). At this time, the leading end of the pole would already be sticking through the other door and well out of the barn. The motion-picture sequence which the pole vaulter might have filmed would confirm the absence of simultaneity as would any other recording instruments which he carried.

Only when we give up our prerelativistic notion that two events can happen at exactly the same time—and that different observers will agree as to what this means—does the world really make sense. Otherwise there would be many paradoxes like the one just presented.

The conclusion of the preceding example will be confirmed with the best possible authorities—beginning with Nobel prize winner Richard P. Feynman, who before his death was a professor of theoretical physics at Caltech: "If we look at the situation carefully we see that events that occur at two separated places at the same time, as seen by Moe in S', do *not* happen at the same time as viewed by Joe in S."[3] Next, another Nobel prize winner—Albert Einstein: "There is no absolute (independent of the space of reference) relation in space, and *no absolute relation in time between two events*"[4] (emphasis added).

This is actually the way God made His universe! There really is no such thing as being at exactly the same time when two different events are separated by a distance.

APPENDIX 4

The Gap Theory

The gap theory places a huge time gap between the first and second verses of Genesis 1. According to this theory, Satan, after rebelling against God long ago, destroyed the earth between the first and second verses of Genesis 1, and God then recreated it in the rest of the chapter. This theory is an old attempt to correlate the supposedly short "days" of Genesis with the antiquity of which science speaks. It is presented in the notes of the Scofield Bible under Isaiah 45:18. Isaiah says:

> For this is what the LORD says—he who created the heavens, he is God; he who fashioned and made the earth, he founded it; he did not create it to be empty, but formed it to be inhabited— . . .
>
> —ISAIAH 45:18

The word "empty" here, and the word "formless" in Genesis 1:2, are both translated from the Hebrew "tohuw." Genesis says that the earth was made "tohuw" (meaning empty, vain, waste, or something like "wild") but Isaiah says that it was not. Obviously one or the other of these verses needs a little bit of interpreting.

What the Scofield Bible did with this pair in its notes was to translate the word "was" in Genesis 1:2 as "became." This is acceptable as far as the Hebrew is concerned. Thus Genesis 1:2 would read, "And the earth *became* without form and void..." So even though God did not *originally* create the earth "tohuw" it later *became* "tohuw" as a result of Satan's fall.

There is a much simpler way to interpret Isaiah. Notice that God did not create the earth "to be empty [tohuw], *but* formed it to be inhabited." What Isaiah means here is easily seen from the comparison between the two states of the earth; Isaiah is contrasting the earth's initial state with the fact that it was later to be inhabited. We see that what is meant by "tohuw" here is "uninhabited"*—or in this particular context "to be uninhabited." Whatever else a person believes, he must accept the fact that the world was uninhabited at the time when God first created it. All that Isaiah 45:18 says is that it was not intended that it should remain that way forever.

This is really a much cleaner way to interpret the Bible. There is no need to hypothesize a giant gap between the first two verses of Genesis—one which God has said nothing about and for which there is no scientific evidence. The scientific account of the universe's creation matches Genesis without any supposed time gap. Furthermore, the Bible says nothing about Satan ever having destroyed the world. We should not assume a theory that does not have either scientific or scriptural support.

---

* The same definition is seen in Jeremiah 4:23-28. The phrase "formless and empty" is elaborated upon in this passage emphasizing the absence of inhabitation, for example, light gone, no people, birds flown away, towns in ruins.

APPENDIX 5

The Ussher Chronology

In this appendix, we will attempt to reconstruct Archbishop James Ussher's A.D. 1650 calculation of the year in which God created Adam. Ussher used the genealogies provided in the Bible to reach a date of 4004 B.C. (As explained in chapter 7, this date does not agree at all with the scientific evidence which would place the first modern men *many* thousands of years earlier.)

King Solomon will serve as a starting point from which to work backward. Solomon was a modern enough figure that he can be tied to history fairly well—at least rough dates are available. Solomon assumed the throne of Israel at about 960 B.C.[1] This date is probably fairly accurate, but in any case it will certainly be accurate enough for the present purpose; after all, this concerns an error of about 30,000 years.

The chronology can be extended backward from Solomon to Adam one step at a time as follows: 1 Kings 6:1 tells us that 480 years elapsed between the time the children of Israel came out of the land of Egypt and the fourth year of Solomon's reign. This means that 476 of those years had elapsed by the year in which Solomon assumed the throne (960 B.C.). So we may conclude that the children of Israel left Egypt 476 years before 960 B.C., or in about the year 1436 B.C.[2]

Next, Exodus 12:40 tells us that the children of Israel stayed in Egypt for 430 years before Moses led them out. From this it can be calculated that the children of Israel entered Egypt about 1866 B.C. This period may include the period preceding the captivity because a shorter span of time is given in Acts 7:6 for the captivity itself.* Presumably this 430-year period in Egypt began when Jacob moved there. This should be at least reasonably close to the actual beginning of that period. (This is an assumption.) As we learn from Genesis 47:28, Jacob had lived in Egypt for 17 years at the time of his death at the age of 147 years. It follows that Jacob's age was 130 years when he moved into Egypt. This means that Jacob was born 130 years before 1866 B.C. or somewhere near the year 1996 B.C.

Next, Genesis 25:26 informs us that Jacob's father, Isaac, was 60 years old when Jacob was born. This puts the birth of Isaac at about 2056 B.C. Similarly, from Genesis 21:5 we find that Abraham was 100 years old when Isaac was born, putting the birth of Abraham at about 2156 B.C.

From this point back to Adam the dates come quite rapidly. Chapters 5 and 11 of Genesis are summarized here:

Genesis 11:10-26:

Terah born 70 years before Abraham . . . . 2226 B.C.[3]

Nahor born 29 years before Terah . . . . 2255 B.C.

Serug born 30 years before Nahor . . . . 2285 B.C.

Reu born 32 years before Serug . . . . 2317 B.C.

Peleg born 30 years before Reu . . . . 2347 B.C.

Eber born 34 years before Peleg . . . . 2381 B.C.

Shelah born 30 years before Eber . . . . 2411 B.C.

Arphaxad born 35 years before Shelah . . . . 2446 B.C.

Shem born 100 years before Arphaxad . . . . 2546 B.C.

---

* See also Acts 13:17-20.

Genesis 5:3-32:

Noah was born 500 years before Shem . . . . 3046 B.C.[4]

Lamech was born 182 years before Noah . . . . 3228 B.C.

Methuselah was born 187 years before Lamech . . . 3415 B.C.

Enoch was born 65 years before Methuselah . . . . . 3480 B.C.

Jared was born 162 years before Enoch . . . . 3642 B.C.

Mahalalel was born 65 years before Jared . . . . 3707 B.C.

Kenan was born 70 years before Mahalalel . . . . 3777 B.C.

Enosh was born 90 years before Kenan . . . . 3867 B.C.

Seth was born 105 years before Enosh . . . . 3972 B.C.

Adam was made 130 years before Seth was born . . 4102 B.C.

Ussher probably used some different verses than these and probably tied them to a different point in history as well. Still, 4102 B.C. agrees well enough with his 4004 B.C. This is where the 6,000-year-old figure for the age of the earth comes from; 4,000 years B.C. plus 2,000 years A.D. adds up to about 6,000 years ago. Actually this calculation does not give the date of the earth's creation—only of Adam's, which was sometime during the sixth "day." And, of course, the Bible does not say how long the "days" of Genesis really were. Still, this chronology provides enough trouble even if it only applies to Adam!

It is considered probable that there are some gaps or possibly even scribal errors in the particular version of the genealogies found in our modern English translations of the Old Testament. A different version of the genealogies is found in the Septuagint (or LXX)—the Greek translation of the Scriptures used by the apostle Luke for his genealogies (Luke 3:23-38), and also by other early church fathers. The LXX genealogies give us 3,412 years between Adam and Abraham instead of the 1,946 years given by our modern translations; this would give us a date of about 5568 B.C. for the creation of

Adam (about 7,500 years ago). Although this would help close the gap, it would not help very much.

Most creationists assume that there are more gaps in the biblical genealogies than even the LXX allows for. Young-earth creationists, for example, usually suggest about 10,000 years for the age of the earth. We are agreed that there remains a discrepancy of thousands of years; the remaining dispute is over just how many thousands.

APPENDIX 6

Was Turning Water into Wine an Example of Creating False Evidence?

The line between hiding the truth and outright deception can sometimes be difficult to discern. For example, when Jesus turned water into wine in John 2:1-11, did he create evidence which bore false witness of the age of that wine? This appendix will investigate that question. What we are told in the second chapter of John is summarized here:

1) A wedding banquet had run out of wine (verse 3).

2) Jesus instructed some servants to fill some jars with water, which they did (verse 7).

3) Jesus instructed those servants to take some of this water to the master of the banquet (verse 8).

4) The master tasted the water which had been turned into wine (verse 9).

5) He did not know where it came from, though the servants did know (verse 9).

6) The master evaluated that wine as "the best" (verse 10).

7) Inferior wine was normally served after the guests had too much to drink (verse 10).

8) This revealed the glory of Jesus (verse 11).

From this sequence of events we might conclude that Jesus had created wine with a false appearance of age and that this somehow revealed his glory—in apparent contradiction to God's truthful nature. Let's take a closer look at the situation.

We will begin with the question of deception: Was anyone deceived? A reader of John is certainly not deceived because he is in on the details. Likewise, we are told that the servants were in on the details. But the master of the banquet was unaware of what had happened and had only his own evaluation of the evidence to go by. His evaluation of the wine was that it was "the best" (we have no reason to doubt him), but did he falsely assume that the wine was old?

We might be tempted to conclude that he made this false assumption because he knew the wine was "the best," and we believe that good wine is aged—or at least that it has every appearance of having been aged. This may be true in our century, but was old wine believed to be good to the ancient Jews —when wine was stored in animal skins instead of glass bottles? In the Bible, "new wine" is consistently represented as being completely adequate in quality. It is the expected material for tithes and offerings, (e.g., Nehemiah 10:39, 13:12). It is a component of blessing (Proverbs 3:10, Joel 3:18), and its removal is an element of cursing (Isaiah 24:7). The term "new wine" also appears to include wine with alcoholic content (Joel 1:5; Acts 2:13,15). The only biblical reference to "old wine" is Luke 5:39, where Jesus says that "no one after drinking old wine wants the new, for he says, 'The old is better.'" Here it is implied that the person's judgment on the matter might have been different if he had not already been drinking old wine.

From the way "new wine" is used in the Bible, we would not expect it to be considered inferior to "old wine" (except possibly in the eyes of those whose judgment is impaired). The master of the banquet in John 2:10 regarded the wine Jesus produced as being "the best" rather than what might be reserved for those whose judgment has become impaired. In the final analysis, it would seem we have no grounds for assuming Jesus produced wine with a false appearance of age. Neither can we be confident that the master of the banquet believed the wine was old. He didn't say it was, and we don't seem to have any clear reason to assume he believed it was old.

We might ask how much alcohol Jesus' wine contained—understanding that it takes at least some time for yeast to turn significant amounts of sugar into alcohol. Unfortunately, we have no way to judge the alcoholic content of Jesus' wine; we are unable to conclusively determine whether or not it was unnaturally high. Again we have no clear way to evaluate whether or not a deception occurred.

Ignoring the issue of age altogether, there is still the fact that the wine tasted like wine—whether it tasted like old wine or new. We have every reason to assume that the master of the banquet believed the wine had come from grapes picked from a vine and not miraculously from water in stone jars. Was this much a deception? Neither we nor the servants were deceived by Jesus, but was the master of the banquet "deceived" because he didn't know the truth? Does Jesus have to tell everyone everything? Or are we expected to sort some things out on our own? 1 Thessalonians 5:21 tells us we are expected to "test everything." Because we have the responsibility to sort truth from error, we cannot accuse Jesus of falsehood just because he doesn't explain everything. A few examples will illustrate this:

God created the earth. At first glance, it looks like it is flat and extends indefinitely. The truth is not immediately obvious, but if we study all of the evidence we are forced to the conclusion that its shape is very close to spherical. God created the stars. At first glance, they appear to be tiny lights attached to the night sky just a few miles away. If we study all of the evidence we are forced to the conclusion that they are each as bright as the sun but that they are many trillions of miles away from us. God created the universe. Our first careless look might suggest to us it is very young or infinitely old; if we study the evidence, we are forced to the conclusion that it is about 10-20 billion years old.

Jesus turned water into wine. At first taste it seemed to match "the best" wine from normal grapes. But if we could take a sample of that wine into a modern biochemistry laboratory, what would it tell us? Would the evidence tell the truth about its origins? God sometimes hides the truth, but when does concealment cross the line and become a lie? How much false evidence is permitted before something becomes a falsehood? I believe that no false evidence is permissible and that God never lies (e.g. Titus 1:2). God's Bible and His creations always speak the truth (e.g., Romans 1:20)—even about their origins. For this reason, I suspect that Jesus' wine would tell the truth—that careful evaluation of all of the evidence would reveal the truth about its age and origin. Anyone is free to disagree with me. Because we do not have a sample of that wine, it would be difficult to prove who is right. However, if we decide God is capable of even this much deception, we can never be certain when God is being completely straight with us and when He isn't. If we accept that God is always completely truthful, it would seem that we must conclude that physical evidence which He creates will ultimately tell us the truth.

BIBLIOGRAPHY

Aardsma, Gerald E., "Has the Speed of Light Decayed?" Institute for Creation Research, I.C.R. Technical Report #1187.

Ackerman, Paul D., *It's a Young World After All, Exciting Evidences for Recent Creation*, © 1986, Baker Book House, Grand Rapids, MI 49506.

Anderson, Marjorie, Ph.D. and Blanche Colton Williams, Ph.D., *Old English Handbook*, © 1935, The Riverside Press, Cambridge.

Asimov, Isaac, *The Early Asimov, Book Two*, © 1972, Fawcett Publications, Inc., Greenwich, CT.

Augustine, St., *The City of God*, an abridged version, from the translation by Gerald G. Walsh, S.J.; Demetrius B. Zema, S.J.; Grace Monahan, O.S.U.; and Daniel J. Honan, 1958, Doubleday, New York.

Austin, Steven A., Ph.D. and D. Russell Humphreys, Ph.D., "The Sea's Missing Salt: A Dilemma for Evolutionists," proceedings of the Second International Conference on Creationism, July 30-August 4, 1990, vol. II, Technical Symposium Sessions and Additional Topics, Creation Science Fellowship, Inc., 362 Ashland Ave., Pittsburgh, PA 15228, pp. 17-33.

Barendsen, G. W., "Yale Natural Radiocarbon Measurements," *Science*, November 1, 1957, vol. 126, no. 3279, p. 911.

Barnes, Thomas G., *Origin and Destiny of the Earth's Magnetic Field*, 1973, Institute for Creation Research, San Diego, CA.

Beiser, Arthur, *Modern Physics: An Introductory Survey*, © 1968, Addison-Wesley Publishing Co. Inc., Reading, MA.

Benditt, John, "Grave Doubts, The Neanderthals May Not Have Buried Their Dead After All," *Scientific American*, June 1989, vol. 260, no. 6, pp. 32,33.

Boardman, William W. Jr. et al., *Science and Creation*, © 1973, Creation-Science Research Center, San Diego, CA.

Breasted, James Henry, *Conquest of Civilization*, © 1926, 1938, The Literary Guild of America, Inc., New York.

Brown, Dr. Walter T. Jr., *In the Beginning . . .*, © 1989, Center for Scientific Creation, 5612 N. 20th Place, Phoenix, AZ 85016.

Calder, Nigel, *Einstein's Universe*, © 1979, The Viking Press, New York.

Chapman, Clark R., "Encounter! Voyager 2 Explores the Uranian System," *The Planetary Report*, March/April 1986, vol. VI, no. 2, pp. 8-12.

Chronic, Halka, *Pages of Stone*, © 1984, The Mountaineers, 306 2nd Avenue West, Seattle, WA 98119.

Chronic, Halka, *Roadside Geology of Utah*, © 1990, Mountain Press Publishing Company, P.O. Box 2399, Missoula, MT 59806.

Cloud, Preston, *Oasis in Space, Earth History from the Beginning*, © 1988, W. W. Norton and Company, New York.

Devore, Jay and Roxy Peck, *Statistics, The Exploration and Analysis of Data*, © 1986, West Publishing, St. Paul, MN.

Einstein, Albert, *The Meaning of Relativity*, © 1945, Princeton University Press, Princeton, NJ.

Einstein, Albert, *Relativity*, © 1931, Crown Publishers, New York.

Feynman, Richard P., *The Feynman Lectures on Physics*, © 1963, Addison-Wesley Publishing Co., Reading, MA, vol. 1.

Fischer, Dick, *The Origins Solution, An Answer in The Creation-Evolution Debate*, © 1996, Fairway Press, Lima, OH.

Garrels, Robert M., and Fred T. Mackenzie, *Evolution of Sedimentary Rocks*, © 1971, W. W. Norton, New York.

Gesenius' Hebrew-Chaldee Lexicon to the Old Testament, © 1979, Baker Book House Co., Grand Rapids, MI.

Gish, Duane T., *Evolution: The Fossils Say No!*, © 1979, Creation-Life Publishers, San Diego, CA.

Goodrick, Edward W., *Do It Yourself Hebrew and Greek*, © 1976, Multnomah Press, Portland, OR 97266.

Gould, Stephen Jay, *Hen's Teeth and Horse's Toes*, © 1983, W. W. Norton and Company, New York.

Gould, Stephen Jay, *The Panda's Thumb*, © 1980, W. W. Norton and Company, New York.

Gowlett, John, *Ascent to Civilization*, © 1984, Alfred A. Knopf, Inc., New York.

Gregory, Stephen A. and Laird A. Thompson, "Superclusters and Voids in the Distribution of Galaxies," *Scientific American*, March 1982, vol. 246, no. 3, p. 106.

Gribbin, John, *Our Changing Planet*, © 1977, Thomas Y. Crowell Company, New York.

Grosvenor, Gilbert M., "Dawn of Humans," supplement to *National Geographic*, February 1997, vol. 191, no. 2.

Guterl, Fred, "Jupiter, Not Bust," *Discover*, January 1997, vol. 18, no. 1, pp. 42-43.

Hafele, J. C. and Richard E. Keating, "Around the World Atomic Clocks: Observed Relativistic Time Gains," *Science*, July 14, 1972, vol. 177, no. 4044, pp. 168-170.

Hafele, J. C. and Richard E. Keating, "Around the World Atomic Clocks: Predicted Relativistic Time Gains," *Science*, July 14, 1972, vol. 177, no. 4044, pp. 166-168.

Hawkes, Jacquetta, *Atlas of Ancient Archaeology*, © 1974, McGraw-Hill Book Company, New York.

Heinze, Thomas F., *Creation vs. Evolution Handbook*, © 1973, Baker Book House, Grand Rapids, MI.

Henbest, Nigel, *Mysteries of the Universe*, © 1981, Van Nostrand Reinhold Company, New York.

Hensley, W. K., et al., "Pressure Dependence of the Radioactive Decay Constant of Beryllium-7," *Science*, September 21, 1973, vol. 181, no. 4105, pp. 1164,1165.

Hintze, Lehi F., *Geologic History of Utah*, © 1988, Brigham Young University, Provo, UT 84602.

Hitch, Charles J., "Dendrochronology and Serendipity," *American Scientist*, May-June 1982, vol. 70, no. 3, pp. 300ff.

Hodge, Paul W., "The Andromeda Galaxy," *Scientific American*, January 1981, vol. 244, no. 1, pp. 92-101.

Horgan, John, "Beyond Neptune," *Scientific American*, October 1995, vol. 273, no. 4, pp. 24,26.

Horne, R. A., *Marine Chemistry*, © 1979, Wiley-Interscience, New York.

Hoyle, Fred and Chandra Wickramasinghe, *Evolution From Space*, © 1981, Simon and Schuster Inc., New York.

Hummel, Charles E., *The Galileo Connection*, © 1986, InterVarsity Press, Downers Grove, IL 60515.

Humphreys, D. Russell, Ph.D., "The Earth's Magnetic Field Is Young," Impact No. 242, *Acts & Facts*, August 1993, vol. 22, no. 8, Institute for Creation Research, El Cajon, CA 92021.

Humphreys, D. Russell, Ph.D., *Starlight and Time*, © 1995, Master Books, Colorado Springs, CO.

Jastrow, Robert, *God and the Astronomers*, © 1978, W. W. Norton and Company, Inc., New York.

Johanson, Donald C., "Face-to-Face with Lucy's Family," *National Geographic,* March 1996, vol. 189, no. 3, pp. 96-117.

Johanson, Donald and Maitland Edey, *Lucy: The Beginnings of Humankind,* © 1981, Warner Books, New York.

Josephus, Flavius, *The Complete Works of Josephus,* © 1960, Kregel Publications, Grand Rapids, MI 49501.

Keith, M. L. and G. M. Anderson, "Radiocarbon Dating: Fictitious Results with Mollusk Shells," *Science,* August 16, 1963, vol. 141, no. 3581, pp. 634ff.

Keller, Phillip, *A Shepherd Looks at Psalm 23,* © 1970, Zondervan Publishing House, Grand Rapids, MI.

Koestler, Arthur, *The Sleepwalkers,* © 1959, The Universal Library, Grosset and Dunlap, New York.

Kofahl, Robert E., Ph.D., *Handy Dandy Evolution Refuter,* © 1977, Beta Books, San Diego, CA.

Kovach, Robert L., Joel S. Watkins, and Pradeep Talwani, "Active Seismic Experiment," *Apollo 16, Preliminary Report,* 1972, NASA SP-315.

Leakey, Richard E., *The Making of Mankind,* © 1981, E. P. Dutton, New York.

Lemonick, Michael B., "Defeat for Strict Creationists," *Time,* June 30, 1986, vol. 127, no. 26. p. 75.

Lerman, A. and M. Meybeck, *Physical and Chemical Weathering in Geochemical Cycles,* © 1988, Kluwer Academic Publishers, Dordrecht, Boston, and London.

Lewin, Roger, *Human Evolution: An Illustrated Introduction,* © 1984, W. H. Freeman and Company, New York.

Lunan, Duncan, *New Worlds for Old,* © 1979, William Morrow and Company, Inc., New York.

Mayer-Gurr, Alfred, *Petroleum Engineering,* © 1976, Ferdinand Enke Publishers, Stuttgart.

McDowell, Josh, and Don Stewart, *Reasons Skeptics Should Consider Christianity,* © 1981, Here's Life Publishers, P.O. Box 1576, San Bernardino, CA 92402.

McKenzie, A. E. E., *A Second Course of Light,* 1956: reprinted 1965, Cambridge University Press, Great Britain.

McMenamin, Mark A. S., "The Emergence of Animals," *Scientific American,* April 1987, vol. 256, no. 4, pp. 94ff.

Menon, Shanti, "Art in Australia, 60,000 years ago," *Discover,* January 1997, vol. 18, no. 1.

Miller, Russell, *Continents in Collision*, © 1983, Time-Life Books, Alexandria, VA.

Milne, Lorus and Margery, *The Audubon Society Field Guide to North American Insects and Spiders*, © 1980, Alfred A. Knopf, Inc., New York.

Morris, Henry M., Ph.D., "Christ and the Time of Creation," Back to Genesis, no. 70, page "a," *Acts & Facts*, October 1994, vol. 23, no. 10, Institute for Creation Research, El Cajon, CA 92021.

Morris, Henry M., *The Genesis Record*, © 1976, Baker Book House, Grand Rapids, MI.

Morris, Henry M., *Scientific Creationism*, © 1974, Master Books, El Cajon, CA.

Nobel, C. S. and J. J. Naughton, "Deep-Ocean Basalts: Inert Gas Content and Uncertainties in Age Dating," *Science*, October 11, 1968, vol. 162, no. 3850, pp. 265ff.

Norman, Trevor and Barry Setterfield, *The Atomic Constants, Light, and Time*," © 1987, Stanford Research Institute International, 333 Ravenswood Ave., Menlo Park, CA 94025.

Norton, O. Richard, *Rocks from Space*, © 1994, Mountain Press Publishing Company, P.O. Box 2399, Missoula, MT 59806.

Numbers, Ronald L., *The Creationists, The Evolution of Scientific Creationism*, © 1992, University of California Press, Berkeley, CA.

Osmer, Patrick S., "Quasars as Probes of the Distant and Early Universe," *Scientific American*, February 1982, vol. 246, no. 2, p. 126.

Parkinson, John H., Leslie V. Morrison, and F. Richard Stephenson, "The Consistency of the Solar Diameter Over the Past 250 Years," *Nature*, December 11, 1980, vol. 288, pp. 548-549.

Press, Frank, and Raymond Siever, *Earth*, © 1974, 1978, 1982, 1986, W. H. Freeman and Company, New York.

Price, George McCready, *The New Geology, A Textbook for Colleges, Normal Schools, and Training Schools; and for the General Reader*, © 1923, Pacific Press Publishing Association, Mountain View, CA.

Renfrew, Colin, "Carbon 14 and the Prehistory of Europe," *Scientific American*, October 1971, vol. 225, no. 4, pp. 63-72.

Ross, Dr. Hugh, *Creation and Time*, © 1994, Navpress Publishing Group, P.O. Box 35001, Colorado Springs, CO 80935.

Ross, Philip E., "Hard Words," *Scientific American*, April 1991, vol. 264, no. 4, pp. 138-147.

Sagan, Carl, *Cosmos*, © 1980, Random House, New York.

Setterfield, Barry, *Geological Time and Scriptural Chronology*, (undated, 1987 or later), available from: Barry Setterfield, Box 318, Blackwood, S.A., 5051 Australia.

Schneider, David, "It's Getting Easier to Find a Date," *Scientific American*, February 1995, vol. 272, no. 2, pp. 18,20.

Schramm, David N. and Gary Steigman, "Particle Accelerators Test Cosmological Theory," *Scientific American*, June 1988, vol. 258, no. 6, pp. 66ff.

Schwarcz, H. P., et al., "ESR dates for the hominid burial site of Qafzeh in Israel," *Journal of Human Evolution*, December 1988, vol. 17, no. 8, pp. 733-737.

Sears, Francis Weston, *Mechanics, Heat, and Sound*, © 1950, Addison-Wesley Publishing Company, Inc., Reading, MA.

Segraves, Kelly L., *And God Created*, vol. 2, © 1973, Creation-Science Research Center, San Diego, CA.

Segre, Emilio, *Annual Review of Nuclear Science*, © 1958, Annual Reviews, Inc., Palo Alto, CA.

Shannon, Foster H., *God Is Light*, © 1981, Green Leaf Press, P.O. Box 5, Campbell, CA 95008.

Shapiro, Robert, *Origins: A Skeptic's Guide to the Creation of Life on Earth*, © 1986, Summit Books, New York.

Shreeve, James, "The Neanderthal Peace," *Discover*, September 1995, vol. 16, no. 9, pp. 70-81.

Smith, David G., *The Cambridge Encyclopedia of Earth Sciences*, © 1981, Crown Publishers Inc./Cambridge University Press, New York.

Spenser, Edmund, *The Faerie Queene*, 1910 edition, J. M. Dent and Sons Ltd., London, and E. P. Dutton & Co. Inc., New York.

Stacey, Frank D., *Physics of the Earth*, © 1969, John Wiley and Sons, Inc., New York.

Strong, James, *Strong's Exhaustive Concordance of the Bible*, Riverside Book and Bible House, Iowa Falls, IA 50126.

Tarling, D. H., *Palaeomagnetism, Principles and Applications in Geology, Geophysics and Archaeology*, © 1983, Chapman and Hall, London.

Taylor, G. Jeffrey, "The Scientific Legacy of Apollo," *Scientific American*, July 1994, vol. 271, no. 1, pp. 40-47.

Thayer, Joseph Henry, D.D., *Thayer's Greek-English Lexicon of the New Testament*, Zondervan Publishing House, Grand Rapids, MI, 1970.

Thompson, Ida, *The Audubon Society Field Guide to North American Fossils*, © 1982, Alfred A. Knopf, Inc., New York.

Turner, Grenville, "Argon-40/Argon-39 Dating of Lunar Rock Samples," *Science,* January 30, 1970, vol. 167, no. 3918, pp. 466ff.

Waechter, John, *Prehistoric Man: The Fascinating Story of Man's Evolution,* © 1977, Octopus Books Limited, London.

Weast, Robert C., Ph.D., *Handbook of Chemistry and Physics, 49th ed.,* © 1964, The Chemical Rubber Company, 18901 Cranwood Parkway, Cleveland, OH, 44128.

Weinberg, Steven, *The First Three Minutes, A Modern View of the Origin of the Universe,* updated ed., © 1977, 1988, Basic Books, Inc., Publishers, New York.

Whitcomb, John C., Th.D. and Henry M. Morris, Ph.D., *The Genesis Flood, The Biblical Record and Its Scientific Implications,* © 1961, The Presbyterian and Reformed Publishing Company.

White, Ellen G., *Early Writings of Ellen G. White,* © 1882, Review and Herald Publishing Association, Hagerstown, MD 21740.

White, Ellen G., *Facts of Faith, in Connection with the History of Holy Men of Old,* © 1864, Review and Herald Publishing Association, Hagerstown, MD 21740.

White, Randall, "Visual Thinking in the Ice Age," *Scientific American,* July 1989, vol. 261, no. 1, p. 92.

Wiseman, P. J., *Ancient Records and the Structure of Genesis,* © 1985, Thomas Nelson Publishers, Nashville, TN.

Woosley, Stan and Tom Weaver, "The Great Supernova of 1987," *Scientific American,* August 1989, vol. 261, no. 2, p. 32.

Wursig, Bernd, "Dolphins," *Scientific American,* March 1979, vol. 240, no. 3. pp. 136-148.

Wysong, Randy L., D.V.M., *The Creation—Evolution Controversy,* © 1976, Inquiry Press, 4925 Jefferson Ave., Midland, MI 48640.

Young, Robert, *Young's Concordance to the Bible,* © 1964, William B. Eerdmans Publishing Company, Grand Rapids, MI.

Youngblood, Ronald, *The Genesis Debate,* © 1986, Thomas Nelson Publishers, Nashville, TN.

"At the Moon Conference: Consensus and Conflict," *Science* NEWS, January 23, 1971, vol. 99, no. 4, p. 62.

"Lunar Sciences: Luna 16, An Unusual Core," *Science* NEWS, January 23, 1971, vol. 99, no. 4, p. 65.

The Soviet-American Conference on Cosmochemistry of the Moon and Planets, 1977, NASA SP-370, vol. 2.

"Velocity of Light 300 Years Ago," *Sky & Telescope,* June 1973, vol. 45, no. 6, pp. 353-354.

Bibles:

The Holy Bible, New International Version, © 1973, 1978, 1984, Zondervan Bible Publishers, Grand Rapids, MI.

The Interlinear Bible, Jay P. Green Sr., © 1976, Baker Book House, Grand Rapids, MI.

The Interlinear Greek-English New Testament, Reverend Alfred Marshall, D. Litt., © 1958, Zondervan Publishing House, Grand Rapids, MI.

The Living Bible, © 1971, Tyndale House Publishers, Wheaton, IL 60187.

The New American Standard Bible, © 1960, Foundation Press Publications, La Habra, CA.

The New Scofield Reference Edition, Holy Bible, Authorized King James Version, ed. C.I. Scofield, D.D., © 1967, Oxford University Press, New York.

The NIV Interlinear Hebrew-English Old Testament, vol. 1, ed. John R. Kohlenberger, © 1979, Zondervan Publishing House, Grand Rapids, MI.

NOTES

Chapter 1: Judging Ourselves First

1. In Romans 7:9, Paul uses "death" in a spiritual or figurative sense. That kind of "death" results when knowledge of the law gives sin an opening. This is different from Adam's death which resulted from his breaking of a law which he had already heard. Although related, Paul's spiritual or figurative death is not quite the same as the death which results from Adam's original sin. We die physically because Adam sinned—whether or not we have heard the law; we do not die in the sense Paul describes until we have heard the commandment.

2. *Gesenius' Hebrew-Chaldee Lexicon to the Old Testament,* © 1979, Baker Book House Co., Grand Rapids, MI, p. 341, entry #3117. According to Gesenius, the primary signification is the heat of the day, but the word is used in a wide variety of ways.

3. Zechariah 14:7 is another example.

4. The NIV Bible translates "yom" as "when" in Genesis 2:17 to make this intended meaning clearer: "... you must not eat from the tree of the knowledge of good and evil, for when you eat of it you will surely die."

5. *The Faerie Queene,* Edmund Spenser, J. M. Dent and Sons Ltd., London, and E. P. Dutton and Co. Inc., New York, 1910 edition, p. 19.

6. *Old English Handbook,* Marjorie Anderson, Ph.D. and Blanche Colton Williams, Ph.D., © 1935, The Riverside Press, Cambridge, p. 140.

7. *Do It Yourself Hebrew and Greek,* Edward W. Goodrick, © 1976, Multnomah Press, Portland, OR 97266, p. 14:6.

8. Ibid., pp. 14:1;15:3,4;16:2,3.

9. Ibid., p. 14:2.

10. *Ancient Records and the Structure of Genesis,* P. J. Wiseman, © 1985, Thomas Nelson Publishers, Nashville, TN, p. 20.

11. Ibid., p. 88.

Chapter 2: Science, Theology, and Truth

1. I will present some predictions of my own in Appendix 1 for those who are interested.

2. In fact, not everything which is lumped under the general heading of psychology is even science! Psychoanalysis, for example, does not follow the rules which would qualify it as a science. See The *Feynman Lectures on Physics*, Richard P. Feynman, © 1963, Addison-Wesley Publishing Co., Reading, MA, vol. 1, p. 3-8.

3. As we have mentioned, there is no rigid rule governing how these terms are to be used. For example, the geological principle of superposition (younger rocks are found above older rocks) is sometimes referred to as a "law" even though there are known exceptions. (Although not strictly true, it is still useful as a general rule.) *The Cambridge Encyclopedia of Earth Sciences*, ed. David G. Smith, Ph.D., © 1981, Crown Publishers Inc./Cambridge University Press, New York, p. 387.

4. But again these terms are sometimes used in different ways. One scientist uses the term "fact" to describe the once-believed inferred generalization of Telegony. Because Telegony was an error, he also uses the term "false fact." *Hen's Teeth and Horse's Toes*, Stephen Jay Gould, © 1983, W. W. Norton & Company, New York, pp. 379-380.

5. It would be more accurate to call these men "scholars" rather than "scientists" because in their day science was not separated from other studies (such as philosophy) as it is in ours. I have used the word "scientists" here because it conveys the correct flavor of my intended meaning better, to my intended readers, than the more correct "scholars" would have.

6. *The Sleepwalkers*, Arthur Koestler, © 1959, The Universal Library, Grosset and Dunlap, New York, p. 603.

7. Proof came in the 1800s in the form of the Foucalt pendulum and the detection of stellar parallax. See *The Galileo Connection*, Charles E. Hummel, © 1986, Inter Varsity Press, Downers Grove, IL 60515, p. 111.

Chapter 3: The Present-Day Stumbling Block

1. This rule also fails for Matthew 8:22. There Jesus said, "Follow me, and let the dead bury their own dead." The same word "dead" ("nekros" in the original New Testament Greek) is used twice in this verse and must mean spiritually dead the first time and physically dead the second time. Otherwise we either have corpses burying the dead or living people being buried.

2. The Old Testament Hebrew writers do not appear to have felt the need for plural forms of either of these words, but English translators do need them. The KJV chose to translate the word "ereb" as "evenings" in Jeremiah 5:6. That word could have been translated very differently; the NIV, for example, translated the same occurrence of "ereb" as "desert," which is also perfectly acceptable. This may sound surprising to us, but our English word "band" could be translated into another language as "ring," "group" or (loosely) "orchestra." Translators must sometimes make decisions between different possibilities based on the context in which words are used.

3. See Isaiah 30:8, *The Interlinear Bible*, Jay P. Green Sr., © 1976, 1979, Baker Book House, Grand Rapids, MI, p. 556.

4. *The Interlinear Greek-English New Testament,* Rev. Alfred Marshall D.Litt., © 1958, Zondervan Publishing House, Grand Rapids, MI, p. 861.

5. For example, the fossilized skeletal remains exist of a large fish from the Cretaceous period (long before man appeared) which had swallowed whole a smaller fish of a different species. See *The Cambridge Encyclopedia of Earth Sciences,* ed. David G. Smith, Ph.D., © 1981, Crown Publishers Inc./Cambridge University Press, New York, p. 369.

6. It is possible to interpret Romans 8:19-22 to disagree with this statement, but it is clear that God's created angels are an exception here as they are not under the "bondage of corruption." Because we must allow for at least this exception, we are unjustified in insisting that animals are included here; they could easily be another exception.

7. As Christians we should have no trouble accepting the truth of this prophecy. God does work miracles. We are assured that one day the lion will eat straw like the ox even though we do not see it happening today. Also, the garden of Eden was a very special place—different in many ways from the rest of the world. While Adam was in the garden, he did not have to cope with thorns and thistles which probably were already created and waiting for him just outside the circle of God's protection (Genesis 3:18).

8. Of course there is no blood involved in the case of plants (see Hebrews 9:22), but see the next argument concerning Jesus. Also, if animals were able to digest plants, this means that at least some laws governing decomposition (decay) were in effect at that time. This means the second law of thermodynamics must have worked then just as it does now; life itself depends on this law.

9. If this inheritance were physical, the laws of genetics predict that only males would inherit Adam's sin. Because we believe otherwise, we must conclude that this would be strictly a spiritual inheritance.

10. *Thayer's Greek-English Lexicon of the New Testament,* Joseph Henry Thayer, D.D., Zondervan Publishing House, Grand Rapids, MI, 1970, p. 363, definition #3.

11. An early scientific version of the old-earth position was proposed during the late 1700s by James Hutton, who argued from geological evidences that God made a durable creation—one capable of replenishing soil which had eroded away. Although Hutton believed God had created the world and would eventually destroy it, he did not believe it would run down on its own. Charles Darwin did not present his theory of evolution until the late 1800s. *Hen's Teeth and Horse's Toes,* Stephen J. Gould, © 1983, W. W. Norton & Company, New York, pp. 84,85.

Chapter 4: A Shadow of Eternity

1. *Handbook of Chemistry and Physics,* 49th ed., ed. Robert C. Weast, Ph.D., © 1964, The Chemical Rubber Company, Cleveland, OH, pp. F-144,145. Unless otherwise indicated, this is the source for the astronomical distances and diameters presented in this chapter. (Distances are center-to-center averages.)

2. "Superclusters and Voids in the Distribution of Galaxies," Stephen A. Gregory and Laird A. Thompson, *Scientific American,* March 1982, vol. 246, no. 3, p. 106.

3. *Mysteries of the Universe,* Nigel Henbest, © 1981, Van Nostrand Reinhold Company, New York, pp. 171-172.

4. M31 is also called NGC 224 in the "New General Catalog." Because it is located in the constellation Andromeda, M31 is sometimes also called the "Andromeda Galaxy."

5. "Superclusters and Voids in the Distribution of Galaxies," Stephen A. Gregory and Laird A Thompson, *Scientific American,* March 1982, vol. 246, no. 3, p. 114.

6. "Quasars as Probes of the Distant and Early Universe," Patrick S. Osmer, *Scientific American,* February 1982, vol. 246, no. 2, p. 126.

7. This actually appears to be suggested as a serious alternative in *Science and Creation,* William W. Boardman Jr., Robert F. Koontz, and Henry M. Morris, © 1973, Creation-Science Research Center, San Diego, CA, p. 26.

8. *A Second Course of Light,* A. E. E. McKenzie M.A., 1956, reprinted 1965, Cambridge University Press, Great Britain, p. 166.

9. *Mysteries of the Universe,* Nigel Henbest, © 1981, Van Nostrand Reinhold Co., New York, pp. 91,170.

10. *The Atomic Constants, Light, and Time,* Trevor Norman and Barry Setterfield, © 1987, Stanford Research Institute International, 333 Ravenswood Ave., Menlo Park, CA 94025. Creationists usually reject theories such as this one, which appeal to changes in the physical constants. It is believed that God must have chosen those constants very carefully for the universe to function correctly. For example, it is cited that "the hydrogen atom could not exist if the mass of the proton was just .2% greater (De Young, 1985)." See "Has the Speed of Light Decayed?" Gerald E. Aardsma, Ph.D., Institute for Creation Research, San Diego, CA, I.C.R. Technical Report no. 1187, p. 1.

11. Their data showed a maximum change of less than 1/2 percent over the past 250 years. This change was approximately equal to the measuring error. *See The Atomic Constants, Light, and Time,* Trevor Norman and Barry Setterfield, p. 26. From this, Setterfield has extrapolated that the speed of light 6,000 years ago was many millions of times its present value. See *Geological Time and Scriptural Chronology,* Barry Setterfield, Box 318, Blackwood, S. A., 5051 Australia, pp. i,vii.

12. *The Atomic Constants, Light, and Time,* Trevor Norman and Barry Setterfield, © 1987, Stanford Research Institute International, 333 Ravenswood Ave., Menlo Park, CA 94025, pp. 9,84.

13. *The Atomic Constants, Light, and Time,* Trevor Norman and Barry Setterfield, © 1987, Stanford Research Institute International, 333 Ravenswood Ave. Menlo Park, CA 94025, p. 26. "Real error" has been added here for comparison; it is the difference between each measurement and light's actual speed—about 299,792,458 meters per second.

14. This effect is not uncommon in scientific inquiry. See "Has the Speed of Light Decayed?" Gerald E. Aardsma, Ph.D., Institute for Creation Research, San Diego, CA, I.C.R. Technical Report no. 1187, p. 2.

15. Ibid., p. 46. A parabola only triples light's speed for 6,000 years ago. The selected curve gives a factor which is millions of times greater. See *Geological Time and Scriptural Chronology*, Barry Setterfield, Box 318, Blackwood, S. A., 5051 Australia, p. vii.

16. Ibid., p. 83.

17. He must travel 3.1416 (pi) times 7927 miles (the earth's equatorial diameter) in 24 hours (the time it takes for the earth to turn a complete circle)—which works out to be about 1037.6 mph (this ignores the correction for sidereal motion).

18. Because light had to make a round trip in Michelson's apparatus, he actually had to measure light traveling in two perpendicular directions. This makes the math more complex but the final result is exactly the same.

19. *Einstein's Universe*, Nigel Calder, © 1979, The Viking Press, New York, p. 105.

20. *Relativity*, Albert Einstein, Ph.D., © 1931, Crown Publishers, New York, pp. 44,117, (acceleration and gravity being equivalent, p. 83).

21. *The Feynman Lectures on Physics*, Richard P. Feynman, © 1963, Addison-Wesley Publishing Co., Reading, MA, p. 15-7.

22. "Around the World Atomic Clocks: Observed Relativistic Time Gains," J. C. Hafele and Richard E. Keating, *Science,* July 14, 1972, vol. 177, no. 4044, pp. 168-170. See also "Around the World Atomic Clocks: Predicted Relativistic Time Gains," J. C. Hafele and Richard E. Keating, *Science,* July 14, 1972, vol. 177, no. 4044, pp. 166-168.

23. *Einstein's Universe*, Nigel Calder, © 1979, The Viking Press, New York, p. 88.

24. *The Meaning Of Relativity*, Albert Einstein, © 1945, 1950, Princeton University Press, Princeton, pp. 30,31. See also The Feynman Lectures on Physics, Richard P. Feynman, © 1963, Addison-Wesley Publishing Co., Reading, MA, vol. 1, p. 15-7.

25. Appendix 3 illustrates this problem of clock synchronization. It examines an interesting paradox which would result if time passed the way we normally supposed it to.

26. This is also true of other universal truths, besides the speed of light, for exactly the same reason. Only those things which are able to have different values to different observers are able to change with time.

27. *Modern Physics: An Introductory Survey*, Arthur Beiser, © 1968, Addison-Wesley Publishing Company, Reading, MA, p. 38. In equation 2-29: $t=t_0/\sqrt{(1-v^2/c^2)}$; if v=c then $t_0=0$ even if "t" is billions of years.

28. *A Shepherd Looks at Psalm 23*, W. Phillip Keller, © 1970, Zondervan, Grand Rapids, Mich., p. 74.

29. As explained, this is true in free space only—light changes speed when it travels through a medium with a different index of refraction than empty space and also when it passes through a gravitational field. The physical world is, at best, a mere shadow of the spiritual reality.

30. "The Great Supernova of 1987," Stan Woosley and Tom Weaver, *Scientific American,* August 1989, vol. 261, no. 2, p. 32.

31. *The Genesis Record,* Henry M. Morris, © 1976, Baker Book House, Grand Rapids, MI, p. 63. Here Morris claims that false apparent age does not suggest deception but is a necessary accompaniment of "genuine" creation. If false appearance of age were really necessary for genuine creation, this would mean God could not create anything slowly or without a false appearance of age. He would be unable to create anything having either true age or true appearance of having been created quickly. (See Appendix 6.)

32. *Hen's Teeth and Horse's Toes,* Stephen Jay Gould, © 1983, W. W. Norton and Company, New York, pp. 201-226.

33. Even in 2 Thessalonians 2:11 where it says, "God sends them a powerful delusion so that they will believe the lie," God does not directly send this delusion Himself. As explained in 2 Thessalonians 2:7-11, the delusion is brought by Satan; God merely stops holding him back. As Psalms 19:1 and Romans 1:20 attest, we see God's handiwork—not Satan's—when we study the creation. (See Appendix 6.)

34. See *Starlight and Time,* D. Russell Humphreys, Ph.D., © 1995, Master Books, Colorado Springs, CO.

Chapter 5: The Testimony of Many Witnesses

1. *Scientific Creationism,* ed. Henry M. Morris, Ph.D., © 1974, Master Books, El Cajon, CA, pp. 136-137.

2. "Dendrochronology and Serendipity," Charles J. Hitch, *American Scientist,* May-June 1982, vol. 70, no. 3, pp. 302-303.

3. Ibid., p. 302.

4. *Pages of Stone,* Halka Chronic, © 1984, The Mountaineers, 306 2nd Avenue West, Seattle, WA 98119, pp. 70-74.

5. The formation is about a mile thick at this location. See *Geologic History of Utah,* Lehi F. Hintze, © 1988, Brigham Young University, Provo, UT 84602, p. 156.

6. These layers—the 42-million-year-old saline tuff and the 44-million-year-old wavy tuff—are both K-Ar datable. See *Geologic History of Utah,* Lehi F. Hintze, © 1988, Brigham Young University, Provo, UT 84602, p. 156 (#41).

7. See, *Physical and Chemical Weathering in Geochemical Cycles,* ed. A. Lerman and M. Meybeck, © 1988, Kluwer Academic Publishers, Dordrecht, Boston, and London. This is calculated from data in the table on p. 272.

8. *Science and Creation,* William W. Boardman Jr. et al., © 1973, Creation-Science Research Center, San Diego, CA, p. 162.

9. Author's note: Isaac Asimov, although a scientist, was never a NASA scientist as might reasonably be inferred from this combination. Originally he was a professor at the Boston University School of Medicine. In 1958 he went full time into freelance writing for the rest of his life. By agreement, he kept his title, Associate Professor of Biochemistry. See *The Early Asimov, Book Two,* Isaac Asimov, © 1972, Fawcett Publications, Inc., Greenwich, CT, p. 300.

10. *Science and Creation,* William W. Boardman Jr. et al., © 1973, Creation-Science Research Center, San Diego, CA, pp. 150-151.

11. *Scientific Creationism,* ed. Henry M. Morris, Ph.D., © 1974, Master Books, El Cajon, CA, pp. 151,152.

12. *The Cambridge Encyclopedia of Earth Sciences,* ed. Davis G. Smith, Ph.D., © 1981, Crown Publishers Inc./Cambridge University Press, New York, p. 33.

13. *The Soviet-American Conference on Cosmochemistry of the Moon and Planets,* 1977, NASA SP-370, vol. 2, pp. 595,659,664.

14. "Lunar Sciences: Luna 16, An Unusual Core," *Science News,* January 23, 1971, vol. 99, no. 4, p. 65.

15. "At the Moon Conference: Consensus and Conflict," *Science News,* January 23, 1971, vol. 99, no. 4, p. 62. *See also The* Soviet-American Conference on Cosmochemistry of the Moon and Planets, 1977, NASA SP-370, vol. 2, p. 664, footnote #2 for a critical evaluation of the Luna 16 depth.

16. "Active Seismic Experiment," Kovach, Robert L., Joel S. Watkins, and Pradeep Talwani, *Apollo 16, Preliminary Report,* 1972, NASA SP-315, pp. 10-1,10-2.

17. *New Worlds for Old,* Duncan Lunan, © 1979, William Morrow and Company, Inc., New York, p. 81.

18. *The Soviet-American Conference on Cosmochemistry of the Moon and Planets,* 1977, NASA SP-370, vol. 2, pp. 571-664. This very technical source was not selected for ease of understanding but to demonstrate just how much work NASA has put into studying the moon's dust.

19. Ibid., p. 574.

20. Another source, "The Scientific Legacy of Apollo", G. Jeffrey Taylor, *Scientific American,* July 1994, vol. 271, no. 1, p. 44, explains that the regolith covers most of the moon's surface to depths as great as 20 meters (about 65 feet).

21. *The Soviet-American Conference on Cosmochemistry of the Moon and Planets,* 1977, NASA SP-370, vol. 2, p. 625.

22. *Scientific Creationism,* ed. Henry M. Morris, Ph.D., © 1974, Master Books, El Cajon, CA, p. 157.

23. Ibid., p. 155. This argument was based on a study purportedly done by geologist Stuart Nevins; the study was actually done by Steven A. Austin, Ph.D., presently with the Institute for Creation Research, who was writing under a false name. For details *see The Creationists, The Evolution of Scientific Creationism,* Ronald L. Numbers, © 1992, University of California Press, Berkeley, CA, p. 280.

24. The average density of the continents is 2.67 g/cc. Therefore, 10 cubic kilometers of continental mass would weigh about 26.7 billion metric tons—or 29.4 billion short tons. See the *Handbook of Chemistry and Physics 49th ed.,* ed. Robert C. Weast, Ph.D., © 1964, The Chemical Rubber Company, Cleveland, OH, p. F-144.

25. *Continents in Collision,* Russell Miller, © 1983, Time-Life Books, Alexandria, VA, pp. 80-82. The world's ocean floors are swept clean by plate motion every 300-400 million years.

26. "Pressure Dependence of the Radioactive Decay Constant of Beryllium-7," W. K. Hensley, et al., *Science,* Sept. 21, 1973, vol. 181, no. 4105, p. 1164.

27. This is how atom bombs work—U-235 which normally has a half-life of 700 million years is made to decay almost instantly in a chain reaction. Still, the only reasonable position concerning fossil artifacts is that the decay rates have been perfectly constant. There is simply no way that billions of years worth of nuclear energy could have been quickly released within the earth in a few thousand years (at least a million times faster than normally) without leaving evidence of that much extra released heat. According to *The Cambridge Encyclopedia of Earth Sciences* (ed. David G. Smith, Ph.D., © 1981, Crown Publishers Inc./Cambridge University Press, New York, p. 151), the earth's radioactive elements normally release 9.5×10^{20} Joules of heat per year. That's a lot of energy—30 million megawatts continuously for 4.5 billion years.

28. For example, argon-40 is produced by potassium which has been around for millions of years, but argon-39 is produced when the same sample is exposed to neutron radiation. "Argon-40/Argon-39 Dating of Lunar Rock Samples," Grenville Turner, *Science,* January 30, 1970, vol. 167, no. 3918, p. 466.

29. *Reasons Skeptics Should Consider Christianity,* Josh McDowell and Don Stewart, © 1981, Here's Life Publishers, P.O. Box 1576, San Bernardino, CA 92402, p. 116.

30. "Yale Natural Radiocarbon Measurements," G. W. Barendsen, *Science,* November 1, 1957, vol. 126, no. 3279, p. 911. See sample Y-159, -1, -2, and the explanation for the preceding sample Y-158.

31. Also, the accuracy of the C-14 method has been greatly improved since this 1957 measurement was made.

32. "Radiocarbon Dating: Fictitious Results with Mollusk Shells," M. L. Keith and G. M. Anderson, *Science,* August 16, 1983, vol. 141, no. 3581, pp. 634-636. 3,000 years seems to represent a maximum limit for this problem in those few situations where it can occur at all.

33. "Carbon 14 and the Prehistory of Europe," Colin Renfrew, *Scientific American,* October 1971, vol. 225, no. 4, pp. 63-72. In particular, see the chart on pp. 66-67.

34. *Ascent to Civilization,* John Gowlett, © 1984, Alfred A. Knopf, Inc., New York, p. 199.

35. Ibid., p. 86.

36. Ibid.

37. Even if some argon does escape, this would make the sample appear younger, not older than it actually was; less argon means less age. Although this will not weaken the present argument, it can still be a problem for scientists. *See Lucy: The Beginnings of Humankind,* Donald Johanson and Maitland Edey, © 1981, Warner Books, New York, pp. 188,192.

38. Actually, the process for potassium-40 is slightly more complicated; there are two different decay mechanisms involved, electron capture into argon-40 and beta decay into calcium-40 (calcium is not normally used in dating samples). There are also other subtleties involved in the decay mechanism; see *Annual Review of Nuclear Science*, ed. Emilio Segre, © 1958, Annual Reviews, Inc., Palo Alto, CA, pp. 261ff.

39. *Lucy: The Beginnings of Humankind*, Donald Johanson and Maitland Edey, © 1981, Warner Books, New York, pp. 190,192.

40. "Deep-Ocean Basalts: Inert Gas Content and Uncertainties in Age Dating," C. S. Noble and J. J. Naughton, *Science*, October 11, 1968, vol. 162, no. 3850, pp. 265-266.

41. *Lucy: The Beginnings of Humankind*, Donald Johanson and Maitland Edey, © 1981, Warner Books, New York, p. 188. Older dates are likely to have greater errors.

42. "Face-to-Face with Lucy's Family," Donald C. Johanson, *National Geographic*, March 1996, vol. 189, no. 3, pp. 113,114.

43. See "It's Getting Easier to Find a Date," David Schneider, *Scientific American*, February 1995, vol. 272, no. 2, pp. 18,20.

44. *Lucy: The Beginnings of Humankind*, Donald Johanson and Maitland Edey, © 1981, Warner Books, New York, p. 116.

45. Ibid., pp. 114-115,152-153. See for examples of contrasting geologies.

46. For example, *Scientific Creationism*, ed. Henry M. Morris, Ph.D., © 1974, Master Books, El Cajon, CA, p. 133.

47. *Lucy: The Beginnings of Humankind*, Donald Johanson and Maitland Edey, © 1981, Warner Books, New York, pp. 95-96.

48. Ibid., pp. 204-206.

49. It's half life is 4.51 billion years, see, *Handbook of Chemistry and Physics 49th Edition*, ed. Robert C. Weast, Ph.D., © 1964, The Chemical Rubber Company, Cleveland, OH, p. B-86.

50. Compare the groundwater assumption of Austin & Humphreys with *Evolution of Sedimentary Rocks*, Robert M. Garrels and Fred T. Mackenzie, © 1971, W. W. Norton, New York, pp 103,104,112.

51. Because very few measurements are involved (less than 20), normal statistical methods give incorrect values; instead, the "Student's" distribution (also called t-curves) must be used which takes into account the larger additional uncertainty arising from small samples. See *Statistics, the Exploration and Analysis of Data*, Jay Devore and Roxy Peck, © 1986, West Publishing, St. Paul, MN, pp. 287,673.

Chapter 6: The Origin of "Scientific Creationism"

1. All of the dates in this chapter concerning the early Christian and Jewish writers were taken from *Creation and Time*, Dr. Hugh Ross, © 1994, Navpress, P.O. Box 35001, Colorado Springs, CO 80935, pp. 16-24.

2. *The Complete Works of Josephus,* Flavius Josephus, © 1960, Kregel Publications, Grand Rapids, MI 49501, p. 25.

3. See *Creation and Time,* Dr. Hugh Ross, © 1994, Navpress, P.O. Box 35001, Colorado Springs, CO 80935, p. 17, for the exact quotation.

4. Ibid., pp. 17,18.

5. Ibid., p. 19. The essence of this argument (based on Hebrews 4:4,6,10) was used back in chapter 3, in the rebuttal to argument 5 concerning God's Sabbath rest.

6. *The City of God,* St. Augustine, Image Books, Doubleday, New York, 1958, pp. 212-214.

7. *Creation and Time,* Dr Hugh Ross, © 1994, Navpress, P.O. Box 35001, Colorado Springs, CO 80935, pp. 16-24.

8. See *Hen's Teeth and Horse's Toes,* Stephen J. Gould, © 1983, W. W. Norton & Company, New York, pp. 84,85.

9. Although I am not an evolutionist, it is not my intent here to address that theory. My views on that subject may be presented in a later book.

10. The statement of Fundamental Beliefs voted by the General Conference of Seventh-day Adventists at Dallas in April, 1980, states: "Seventh-day Adventists accept the Bible as their only creed ... We do not believe that the writings of Ellen White may be used as the basis of doctrine."

11. *Facts of Faith, in Connection with the History of Holy Men of Old,* White, Ellen G., Steam Press, Battle Creek MI, © 1864, pp. 90,91.

12. *Early Writings of Ellen G. White,* White, Ellen G., Review and Herald Publishing Association, Hagerstown, MD 21740, © 1882, pp. 216,217.

13. This amounted to some elementary courses in some of the natural sciences. See *The Creationists, the Evolution of Scientific Creationism,* Ronald Numbers, © 1992, University of California Press, Berkeley, CA, p. 75.

14. Ibid., pp. 75,76.

15. *Facts of Faith, in Connection with the History of Holy Men of Old,* White, Ellen G., Steam Press, Battle Creek MI, © 1864, pp. 78,79.

16. *The New Geology, A Textbook for Colleges, Normal Schools, and Training Schools; and for the General Reader,* Price, George McCready, © 1923, Pacific Press Publishing Association, Mountain View, CA, p. 465.

17. For example, although two-thirds of the world's oil reserves are located in the Mideast, the area does not contain a significant fraction of the world's coal. See *Earth,* Frank Press and Raymond Siever, © 1974, 1986, W. H. Freeman and Company, New York, pp. 581,586.

18. *The New Geology, A Textbook for Colleges, Normal Schools, and Training Schools; and for the General Reader,* Price, George McCready, © 1923, Pacific Press Publishing Association, Mountain View, CA, p. 71.

19. *The Genesis Flood, the Biblical Record and Its Scientific Implications,* Whitcomb, John C., Th.D. and Henry M. Morris, Ph.D., © 1961, The Presbyterian and Reformed Publishing Company.

20. Ibid., p. 277.

21. Ibid., p. 435.

22. See *The Creationists, the Evolution of Scientific Creationism,* Ronald Numbers, © 1992, University of California Press, Berkeley, CA, p. 198,199.

23. Ibid., pp. 202,204.

24. See, *The Genesis Flood, the Biblical Record and Its Scientific Implications,* Whitcomb, John C., Th.D. and Henry M. Morris, Ph.D., © 1961, The Presbyterian and Reformed Publishing Company, pp. 279-281,327.

25. See *Geologic History of Utah,* Lehi F. Hintze, © 1988, Brigham Young University, Provo, UT 84602, p. 196.

26. Ibid., p. 193.

27. See *Roadside Geology of Utah,* Halka Chronic, © 1990, Mountain Press Publishing Company, P.O. Box 2399, Missoula, MT 59806, pp. 86,298.

28. *The Creationists, the Evolution of Scientific Creationism,* Ronald Numbers, © 1992, University of California Press, Berkeley.

Chapter 7: Understanding Genesis Chapter One

1. See also Hebrews 11:3, "... the universe was formed at God's command."

2. Although discovery of the equivalence between matter and energy (E=mc2) is universally attributed to Albert Einstein, not all sources agree. See *Evolution from Space,* Fred Hoyle and Chandra Wickramasinghe, © 1981, Simon & Schuster Inc., New York, p. 10.

3. *Mechanics, Heat, and Sound,* Francis Weston Sears, © 1950, Addison-Wesley Publishing Company, Inc., Reading, MA, p. 464.

4. *God and the Astronomers,* Robert Jastrow, © 1978, W. W. Norton and Company, Inc., New York, p. 47

5. Compounding the roughness and incompleteness of Hubble's early measurements was the fact that one of his assumptions was also in error. See "The Andromeda Galaxy" Paul W. Hodge, *Scientific American,* January 1981, vol. 244, no. 1, pp. 95-96.

6. *God and the Astronomers,* Robert Jastrow, © 1978, W. W. Norton and Company, Inc., New York, pp. 14-21

7. "Particle Accelerators Test Cosmological Theory," David N. Schramm and Gary Steigman, *Scientific American,* June 1988, vol. 258, no. 6, pp. 68,69.

8. Those who are uncomfortable with a moment of creation (and hence a creator) have proposed the hypothesis that the universe goes through endless cycles of "big bang" followed by "big crunch" where it collapses again only to be reexploded in a

subsequent "big bang." Even if this hypothesis proves to be true, it does not eliminate the need for a moment of creation anyway because even these cycles will run down; each successive cycle is believed to be comprised of less matter and more energy than the preceding one. See *The First Three Minutes, A Modern View of the Origin of the Universe*, updated ed., Steven Weinberg, © 1977, 1988, Basic Books, Inc., Publishers, New York, pp. 153-154.

9. See *Einstein's Universe*, Nigel Calder, © 1979, The Viking Press, New York, pp. 122,124-125.

10. *Gesenius' Hebrew-Chaldee Lexicon to the Old Testament*, © 1979, Baker Book House Co., Grand Rapids, MI, p. 81, entry #776, definition #6.

11. *Mysteries of the Universe*, Nigel Henbest, © 1981, Van Nostrand Reinhold Co., New York, p. 175.

12. Ibid., pp. 14,15,88,89.

13. This conclusion is based on the relative abundance of the various elements of the periodic table as they occur in our planetary system. Einstein's Universe, Nigel Calder, © 1979, The Viking Press, New York, p. 17.

14. *Gesenius' Hebrew-Chaldee Lexicon to the Old Testament*, © 1979, Baker Book House Co., Grand Rapids, MI, p. 766, entry #7363.

15. See *The Genesis Debate*, Ronald Youngblood, © 1986, Thomas Nelson Publishers, Nashville, TN, pp. 113-118, the "no" argument. Also, the Hebrew grammatical structure of this verse suggests that "God" should be the subject and the word here translated "spirit" (or breath or wind) should have been the verb. The word here translated "moved" is preceded by the Hebrew letter "mem" which suggests the preposition for "from" or "out of." (See, *Do It Yourself Hebrew and Greek*, Edward W. Goodrick, © 1976, Multnomah Press, Portland OR 97266. p. 16:3.) The word could possibly have been translated something like "from moving" or "as a result of moving." This suggests a translation like, "And God blew/breathed from/by moving on the face of the waters."

16. *Origins: A Skeptic's Guide to the Creation of Life on Earth*, Robert Shapiro, © 1986, Summit Books, New York, p. 96.

17. *God and the Astronomers*, Robert Jastrow, © 1978, W. W. Norton and Company, Inc., New York, pp. 106-107. The temperature at which a star will kindle is 20 million degrees Fahrenheit.

18. As mentioned earlier, size determines whether a body will ultimately become a hot star or a cool planet. See *Mysteries of the Universe*, Nigel Henbest, © 1981, Van Nostrand Reinhold Co., New York, p. 93.

19. For this theory, see *Origins: A Skeptic's Guide to the Creation of Life on Earth*, Robert Shapiro, © 1986, Summit Books, New York, p. 96. Another theory is that a geological upheaval stripped the original atmosphere: *The Cambridge Encyclopedia of Earth Sciences*, ed. David G. Smith, Ph.D., © 1981, Crown Publishers Inc./Cambridge University Press, New York, p. 260.

20. Proverbs 8:23,24 seems to provide a possible (although easily disputable) mention of such a moment: "I [wisdom] was appointed from eternity, from the beginning, before the world began. When there were no oceans, I was given birth, ..."

21. *Marine Chemistry,* R. A. Horne, © 1969, Wiley-Interscience, New York, p. 421.

22. See *Oasis in Space, Earth History from the Beginning,* Preston Cloud, © 1988, W. W. Norton & Company, New York, p. 122. See also *The Panda's Thumb,* S. J. Gould, © 1980, W. W. Norton & Company, New York, p. 218.

23. The radioactive uranium, thorium, and potassium in the earth's interior are estimated to produce about 9.5x1020 Joules/year of heat energy. This is sufficient to keep it quite warm. See *The Cambridge Encyclopedia of Earth Sciences,* ed. David G. Smith, Ph.D., © 1981, Crown Publishers Inc./Cambridge University Press, New York, p. 151.

24. The original water was volcanic steam. After the earth cooled, this steam condensed into surface water. See *Marine Chemistry,* R. A. Horne, © 1969, Wiley-Interscience, New York, p. 421.

25. Deeps, as in deep waters, *Gesenius' Hebrew-Chaldee Lexicon to the Old Testament,* © 1979, Baker Book House Co., Grand Rapids, MI, p. 857, entry #8415.

26. Ibid., p. 780, entry #7549.

27. Ibid., p. 780, entry #7554.

28. See *Origins: A Skeptic's Guide to the Creation of Life on Earth,* Robert Shapiro, © 1986, Summit Books, New York, p. 93.

29. See *The Cambridge Encyclopedia of Earth Sciences,* ed. David G. Smith, Ph.D., © 1981, Crown Publishers Inc./Cambridge University Press, New York, pp. 161,162.

30. See *Continents in Collision,* Russell Miller, © 1983, Time-Life Books, Alexandria, VA, pp. 43,129.

31. Ibid., pp. 143,162.

32. *The Audubon Society Field Guide to North American Fossils,* Ida Thompson, Alfred A. Knopf, New York, pp. 759-761.

33. See *Oasis in Space, Earth History from the Beginning,* Preston Cloud, © 1988, W. W. Norton and Company, New York, pp. 369,375-376.

34. *Scientific Creationism,* ed. Henry M. Morris, Ph.D., © 1974, Master Books, El Cajon, CA, p. 227.

35. *The Cambridge Encyclopedia of Earth Sciences,* ed. David G. Smith, Ph.D., © 1981, Crown Publishers Inc./Cambridge University Press, New York, p. 383. This source explains that the poor fossilability of plants leads to erroneous conclusions about their history. See also *Human Evolution: An Illustrated Introduction,* Roger Lewin, © 1984, W. H. Freeman and Company, New York, p. 59, for an example of a situation where plant matter was believed to have been present yet has produced no fossil evidence.

36. See *The Cambridge Encyclopedia of Earth Sciences,* ed. David G. Smith, Ph.D., © 1981, Crown Publishers Inc./Cambridge University Press, New York, p. 325.

37. See *The Panda's Thumb*, S. J. Gould, © 1980, W. W. Norton & Company, New York, p. 219.

38. See *The Cambridge Encyclopedia of Earth Sciences*, ed. David G. Smith, Ph.D., © 1981, Crown Publishers Inc./Cambridge University Press, New York, pp. 261,262.

39. *Our Changing Planet*, John Gribbin, © 1977, Thomas Y. Crowell Company, New York, p. 12.

40. See *The Cambridge Encyclopedia of Earth Sciences*, ed. David G. Smith, Ph.D., © 1981, Crown Publishers Inc./Cambridge University Press, New York, p. 374. Oxygen atoms are released by plants—aquatic or otherwise.

41. See *Origins: a Skeptic's Guide to the Creation of Life on Earth*, Robert Shapiro, © 1986, Summit Books, New York, p. 92.

42. Ibid., p. 93. It is difficult to know how much protection the thick clouds which were surrounding the earth at this time might have provided; it probably would not have been significant though.

43. See *Oasis in Space, Earth History from the Beginning*, Preston Cloud, © 1988, W. W. Norton and Company, New York, p. 327.

44. Ibid.

45. Gesenius' Hebrew-Chaldee Lexicon to the Old Testament, © 1979, Baker Book House, MI, p. 81, entry #776.

46. *The Genesis Record*, Henry M. Morris, © 1976, Baker Book House, Grand Rapids, MI, p. 63. See also *The Creation-Evolution Controversy*, Randy L. Wysong, © 1976, Inquiry Press, 4925 Jefferson Ave., Midland, MI 48640, p. 57.

47. *The Panda's Thumb*, Stephen Jay Gould, © 1980, W. W. Norton & Company, New York, pp. 182-184.

48. See "The Scientific Legacy of Apollo", G. Jeffrey Taylor, *Scientific American*, July 1994, vol. 271, no. 1, p. 43.

49. At that time a day-night cycle would have lasted considerably less than 24 hours. The earth's rotation has slowed down since then. See *The Panda's Thumb*, Stephen Jay Gould, © 1980, W. W. Norton and Company, New York, pp. 316,319.

50. See *The NIV Interlinear Hebrew-English Old Testament*, ed. John R. Kohlenberger III, © 1979, Zondervan Publishing House, Grand Rapids, MI, vol. 1, p. 2, verse 16.

51. Another possibility to consider is that "made" could be translated "had made" (as it sometimes is, such as in Genesis 2:8,9). See *The Genesis Debate*, Ronald Young-blood, © 1986, Thomas Nelson Publishers, Nashville, TN, p. 38, the "no" argument; pp. 45-46, the "yes" argument.

52. *Gesenius' Hebrew-Chaldee Lexicon to the Old Testament*, © 1979, Baker Book House Co., Grand Rapids, MI, p. 138, entry #1254.

53. Ibid., pp. 657,658, entry #6213.

54. The Hebrew examples and statistics used in this chapter are based on the KJV and are from *Young's Concordance to the Bible,* Robert Young LL.D., © 1964, William B. Eerdmans Publishing Company, Grand Rapids, MI.

55. The Hebrew suggests the alternate reading "two of the great lights." *See The NIV Interlinear Hebrew-English Old Testament,* ed. John R. Kohlenberger III, © 1979, Zondervan Publishing House, Grand Rapids, MI, vol. 1, p. 2, verse 16.

56. *Gesenius' Hebrew-Chaldee Lexicon to the Old Testament,* © 1979, Baker Book House, MI, pp. 572-574, entry #5414.

57. This was modeled after *The NIV Interlinear Hebrew-English Old Testament,* ed. John R. Kohlenberger III, © 1979, Zondervan Publishing House, Grand Rapids, MI, vol. 1, p. 2.

58. See "The Emergence of Animals," Mark A. S. McMenamin, *Scientific American,* April 1987, vol. 256, no. 4, pp. 94ff.

59. *Gesenius' Hebrew-Chaldee Lexicon to the Old Testament,* © 1979, Baker Book House, MI, p. 614, entry #5775.

60. *The Hebrew-Chaldee Lexicon to Strong's Exhaustive Concordance of the Bible,* James Strong S.T.D., LL.D., Riverside Book and Bible House, Iowa Falls, IA 50126. Entry #5775.

61. Cockroaches are among the oldest winged insects—appearing 350 million years ago. (They can and do occasionally fly!) *See The Audubon Society Field Guide to North American Insects and Spiders,* Lorus and Margery Milne, © 1980, Alfred A. Knopf, Inc., New York, p. 391.

62. This particular date has been one of the most hotly contested potassium-argon dates ever. Still the most wildly variant dates fall more or less within the 2-3 million year age range. *Lucy: The Beginnings of Humankind,* Donald C. Johanson and Maitland A. Edey, © 1981, Warner Books, New York, pp. 238-243.

63. *Ascent to Civilization,* John Gowlett, © 1984, Alfred A. Knopf, Inc., New York, p. 60.

64. Ibid., p. 104.

65. *Atlas of Ancient Archaeology,* Jacquetta Hawkes, © 1974, McGraw-Hill Book Company, New York, p. 197.

66. *Ascent to Civilization,* John Gowlett, © 1984, Alfred A. Knopf, Inc., New York, p. 118.

67. For example, see *Handy Dandy Evolution Refuter,* Robert E. Kofahl, © 1977, Beta Books, San Diego, CA, pp. 74-75.

68. See "The Neanderthal Peace," James Shreeve, *Discover,* September 1995, vol. 16, no. 9, pp. 78-80. This article attempts to answer the question of how the Neanderthals and moderns lived in the same place at the same time, for tens of thousands of years, yet left no evidence of successful interbreeding. However, the very obscure statements found in Genesis 6:2-4 might suggest at least infertile crosses.

69. Sources disagree as to whether the size of the Neanderthal's brain was, on the average, larger or smaller than modern man's. According to *Prehistoric Man: The*

Fascinating Story of Man's Evolution, John Waechter, © 1977, Octopus Books Limited, London, p. 60, their average brain size was 300 cc. smaller than ours and was much less developed in terms of surface area. A more recent source, *Human Evolution: An Illustrated Introduction,* Roger Lewin, © 1984, W. H. Freeman Co., New York, pp. 72,73, claims that the Neanderthals had slightly larger (by about 40 cc.) brains than ours; here the "extra" capacity is thought to be for control of their extra muscles.

70. "Dolphins," Bernd Wursig, *Scientific American,* March 1979, vol. 240, no. 3. pp. 136,140,146.

71. It could be argued that the biggest advantage we have over dolphins is not our brains but our hands. Of course this statement is extremely anthropocentric (viewed only in terms of human values). A porpoise might not regard our hands as sufficient compensation for our lack of sonar-related abilities.

72. *The Making of Mankind,* Richard E. Leakey, © 1981, E. P. Dutton, New York, p. 150. This source makes the assumption of clothing based on the cold habitat. See also *Prehistoric Man: The Fascinating Story of Man's Evolution,* John Waechter, © 1977, Octopus Books Limited, London, p. 57, for the same reasoning.

73. *Human Evolution: An Illustrated Introduction,* Roger Lewin, © 1984, W. H. Freeman and Company, New York, p. 53. This source says that it is not known when the short, fine hair of modern humans appeared.

74. *Ascent to Civilization,* John Gowlett, © 1984, Alfred A. Knopf, Inc., New York, p. 123. See for earliest known sewing tools. See also Prehistoric Man: The Fascinating Story of Man's Evolution, John Waechter, © 1977, Octopus Books Limited, London, pp. 63,65. The first evidence of clothing was preserved only by ornamental beads.

75. *Ascent to Civilization,* John Gowlett, © 1984, Alfred A. Knopf, Inc., New York, p. 128. Possibly the oldest example of "art" is a collection of circular depressions in Australian sandstone dated about 60,000 years ago. See, "Art in Australia, 60,000 Years Ago," Shanti Menon, *Discover,* January 1997, vol. 18, no. 1, pp. 33,34. Whether or not these depressions really constitute "art" might be disputed, but the evidence tells us they were at least deliberately constructed.

76. "Grave Doubts, The Neanderthals may not have buried their dead after all," John Benditt, *Scientific American,* June 1989, vol. 260, no. 6, pp. 32,33.

77. "Hard Words," Philip E. Ross, *Scientific American,* April 1991, vol. 264, no. 4, p. 147.

78. "ESR dates for the hominid burial site of Qafzeh in Israel," H. P. Schwarcz et al., *Journal of Human Evolution,* December 1988, vol. 17, no. 8, pp. 733-734. See also "The Neanderthal Peace," James Shreeve, *Discover,* September 1995, vol. 16, no. 9, p. 76; and, "Visual Thinking in the Ice Age," Randall White, *Scientific American,* July 1989, vol. 261, no. 1, p. 92. There are also genetic arguments which place the age of modern man somewhere in the 50-250 thousand-year range. Genetic arguments are based on mathematical analysis of the mitochondrial DNA of living people. Such arguments are not yet considered very reliable. If an intelligent creator has been methodically modifying DNA, perhaps in several female

individuals for each new species (Eve, Cain's wife ...), then the method encounters an unexpected difficulty which would make it nearly useless.

79. "Dawn of Humans," Gilbert M. Grosvenor, chairman, *National Geographic,* February 1997, vol. 191, no. 2.

80. "Ussher" is also correctly spelled "Usher."

81. Luke's genealogies follow those listed in the Septuagint or LXX, the Greek translation of the Hebrew Scriptures which was commonly used during his day.

82. *Evolution: the Fossils Say No!,* Duane T. Gish, Ph.D., © 1979, Creation-Life Publishers, San Diego, CA, p. 60.

83. *Scientific Creationism,* ed. Henry M. Morris, Ph.D., © 1974, Master Books, El Cajon, CA, p. 250.

84. For example, according to Egyptologist James Henry Breasted, the Egyptians invented the 365-day calendar in the year 4236 B.C. See The Conquest of Civilization, James Henry Breasted, © 1926, 1938, The Literary Guild of America, Inc., New York, p. 56. This date is not directly tied to historic records but was calculated relative to an astronomical observation concerning a more recent, but purportedly mathematically related, event. Also ancient Chinese family's genealogies predate Ussher's creation date. See *Continents in Collision,* Russell Miller, © 1983, Time-Life Books, Alexandria, VA, p. 10.

85. This theory was first brought to my attention by the book, *God Is Light,* Foster H. Shannon, © 1981, Green Leaf Press, P.O. Box 5, Campbell, CA 95008, p. 51. More recently, a very thorough and persuasive development of this idea was presented in, *The Origins Solution, An Answer in the Creation-Evolution Debate,* Dick Fischer, © 1996, Fairway Press, Lima OH. The Bible calls Adam the first man (1 Corinthians 15:45) but it also calls Jesus the "Last Adam." This tends to imply that something else besides "the absolute first man" may have been intended. Acts 17:26 and Romans 5:12 suggest additional arguments which this theory must address before it should be given credence. If it turns out that this theory is the truth, we must still consider the fact that some of those other men wore clothes. This would separate them from the other apelike creatures; it would seem that they must also have had a knowledge of sin. Perhaps something like this is what the very obscure mention of "the sons of God" in Genesis 6:2 refers to, but for the moment this is all speculation.

Chapter 8: Repairing the Damage

1. *Hen's Teeth and Horse's Toes,* Stephen Jay Gould, © 1983, W. W. Norton & Company, New York, p. 259.

Appendix 3:

1. *See Modern Physics: An Introductory Survey,* Arthur Beiser, © 1968, Addison-Wesley Publishing Co. Inc., Reading, MA, pp. 35,36. The equation we are using is identified as "2-28" at the bottom of page 36.

2. Ibid., p. 29.

3. *The Feynman Lectures on Physics,* Richard P. Feynman, © 1963, Addison-Wesley Publishing Co., Reading, MA vol. 1, p. 15-7.

4. *The Meaning of Relativity,* Albert Einstein, © 1945, 1950, Princeton University Press, Princeton, NJ, pp. 30,31.

Appendix 5:

1. *The Conquest of Civilization,* James Henry Breasted, © 1926, 1938, The Literary Guild of America, Inc., New York, p. 187. (This event was synchronous with the death of King David.) Other sources give 971 B.C. which only differs by eleven years.

2. There are two main theories concerning the time of the Exodus. The earlier date is c. 1445-1440 B.C., during the reign of Amenhotep, the later is c. 1290 B.C. during the reign of Raamses II. See *The Origins Solution, An Answer in the Creation-Evolution Debate,* Dick Fischer, © 1996, Fairway Press, Lima, OH, p. 325. Our calculation agrees very well with the earlier date, and is within 146 years of the later date.

3. Actually Genesis 11:26 says, "After Terah had lived 70 years, he became the father of Abram, Nahor and Haran." The three were probably each born in different years. Although Abram is listed first (being the most important from the Jewish perspective), it appears from other Scripture that he was not actually the first born of the three. Genesis 11:32 tells us that Terah died in Haran at the age of 205. We see from Acts 7:4 that Abram (Abraham) moved from Haran to Israel only after Terah died. And finally Genesis 12:4 tells us that Abram was 75 when he left Haran. This means that Terah must have been about 130 (or older) when Abram was born. This introduces a 60-year (or greater) error to the traditional chronology.

4. Here, in Genesis 5:32, the text says, "After Noah was 500 years old, he became the father of Shem, Ham and Japheth." It is improbable that all three were born within the same year. There are clues as to exactly when Shem was born. Genesis 11:10 says that when Shem begat Arphaxad he was 100 years old and that Arphaxad was born two years after the flood. This means that Shem was 98 when the flood ended. Genesis 8:13 tells us that the flood ended when Noah was 601. Noah would have to have been about 503 when Shem was born if he were to be 601 years old when Shem was 98. This introduces only a three-year error.

Scripture Index

Primary references are italicized.

OLD TESTAMENT

Topical Index

Primary references are italicized.